C000084401

The Beauties of History; Or, Pictures of Virtue and Vice, Drawn from Real Life
by L M. Stretch

Address:
HardPress
8345 NW 66TH ST #2561
MIAMI FL 33166-2626
USA
Email: info@hardpress.net

2212 $f.$ 3

THE
BEAUTIES
OF
HISTORY;
OR,
PICTURES OF VIRTUE AND VICE, DRAWN FROM REAL LIFE;
DESIGNED
For the Instruction and Entertainment of Youth.

By L. M. STRETCH.

among the books ___ of Lesale

given by B——one of her friends.

PARIS:

Printed for VERGANI, Quai de l'Horloge du Palais, n°. 28, près le Pont-au-Change.

THE NINTH YEAR.

CONTENTS.

AFFECTION CONJUGAL.

SENTIMENTS.   Page 1
EXAMPLES.

In the wife of Julius Sabinus   2
The young prince of Armenia to the
  princess   5

AFFECTION PARENTAL.

SENTIMENTS.   6
EXAMPLES,

In Solon the philosopher   7
Cornelia, the mother of the Gracchi   8

AFFECTION FILIAL.

SENTIMENTS.   9
EXAMPLES,

In Young Manlius, son of the Roman
  dictator   11
Antigonus to Demetrius, king of Ma-
  cedon   13
Demetrius to his father   14
The son of Metellus   15
Epaminondas the Grecian general   16

AFFECTION FRATERNAL.

SENTIMENTS.   17
EXAMPLES,

In Darius king of Persia   18
The three sons of the king of Cucho   22

a ij

AMBITION.

SENTIMENTS.   24

EXAMPLES.

In M. Manlius thrown from the capitol
which he had saved   25

The various fortunes of Marius the famous Roman   27

BENEFICENCE.

SENTIMENTS.   35

EXAMPLES,

In Acaces bishop of Amida   36

The restoration of the island of Rhodes   37

CLEMENCY.

SENTIMENTS.   40

EXAMPLES,

In The Syracusians towards Deucetius ,
the Sicilian chief   ib.

The noble speech of Nicolaus   43

COMPASSION.

SENTIMENTS.   47

EXAMPLES,

In Alexander the Great   ib.

CONSCIENCE.

SENTIMENTS.   51

EXAMPLES,

In The caliph Montaser   ib.

A jeweller   52

CONSTANCY.

SENTIMENTS.   55

EXAMPLE,

In Regulus the Roman general   56

Contents. v

CONTINENCE.
SENTIMENTS. 61
EXAMPLE,
In Scipio 62

COURAGE.
SENTIMENTS. 68
EXAMPLES,
In P. Horatius 69
Jane of Flanders , wife of Charles de Blois 71

DISINTERESTEDNESS.
SENTIMENTS. 75
EXAMPLES,
In Phocion 76
Hæphestion 77
Chevalier Bayard 80

DRUNKENNESS.
SENTIMENTS. 82
EXAMPLES,
Very agreeably exposed by Cyrus the Great , when a youth ib.
In Clitus , the friend of Alexander the Great 86

EQUITY.
SENTIMENTS. 89
EXAMPLES,
In the Roman senate 90
Trajan the Roman emperor 91
The Persians 93

FLATTERY.
SENTIMENTS. 95
EXAMPLES,
In Conon to Ptolomy 96

Antiochus Sidetes 98
The courtiers of Canute the Great 99

FREEDOM with Great Men dangerous.
Sentiments. 101
Examples,
In Alexander the Great 102
Darius 107
Description of his magnificent army, and the defeat of it 111

FRIENDSHIP.
Sentiments. 115
Example,
In Alcander and Septimius 118

GENEROSITY.
Sentiments. 125
Example,
In Camillus 126

HAPPINESS.
Sentiments. 131
Example,
In Crœsus 132

INDUSTRY.
Sentiments. 139
Examples,
In Demosthenes 140
Lysander 145

INGRATITUDE.
Sentiments. 147
Examples,
In a Macedonian soldier 148
Xenocrates 150

J U S T I C E.

S E N T I M E N T S.   151
E X A M P L E S,
In Aristides   152

L U X U R Y.

S E N T I M E N T S.   156
E X A M P L E S,
In the Persians   157
   Scythians   164
   Athenians   165
   Romans   ib.
   Reflections   ib.

M A G I S T R A T E.

S E N T I M E N T S.   166
E X A M P L E,
In Glauco and Socrates   167

M A G N A N I M I T Y.

S E N T I M E N T S.   171
E X A M P L E S,
In a Privernian prisoner   ib.
   Porus, an Indian prince   173

P A T I E N C E.

S E N T I M E N T S.   174
E X A M P L E S,
In Tiberius   176
   Epitectus   177
   Socrates   ib.

P A T R I O T I S M.

S E N T I M E N T S.   182
E X A M P L E S,
In Alexander the Roman emperor   183
   Brutus   185

P O L I T E N E S S.

S e n t i m e n t s.   189
E x a m p l e s,

In Honorius   190
    Garcia   193
    The character of a fine gentleman   196

P R I D E.

S e n t i m e n t s.   197
E x a m p l e s,

In Alexander   199
    Menecrates   201

P R O D I G A L I T Y.

S e n t i m e n t s.   202
E x a m p l e s,

In Heliogabalus   204
    Cleopatra   206

R E V E N G E.

S e n t i m e n t s.   210
E x a m p l e s,

In Alexander   211
    Aliverdi   213

T R E A C H E R Y.

S e n t i m e n t s.   215
E x a m p l e s,

In Caracalla   *ib.*
    Antigonus   216

W E A L T H, C o n t e m p t o f.

S e n t i m e n t s.   218
E x a m p l e s,

In Philopœmen   220
    Fabricius   222
    Valerius Publicola   229

THE
BEAUTIES
OF
HISTORY.

AFFECTION CONJUGAL.

SENTIMENTS.

OF all the pleasures that endear human life, there are none more worthy the attention of a rational creature than those that flow from the mutual return of conjugal love.

When two minds are thus engaged by the ties of reciprocal sincerity, each alternately receives and communicates a transport that is inconceivable to all but those who are in this situation: hence arises that heart-ennobling solicitude for one another's welfare; that tender sympathy which alleviates affliction, and that participated pleasure which heightens prosperity and joy itself.

A good wife makes the cares of the world sit easy, and adds a sweetness to its pleasures: she is a man's best companion in pros-

A

perity , and his only friend in adversity ; the carefullest preserver of his health , and the kindest attendant on his sickness : a faithful adviser in distress , a comforter in affliction , and a prudent manager of all his domestic affairs.

Good—nature and evenness of temper will give you an easy companion for life ; virtue and good sense an agreeable friend ; love and constancy a good wife or husband.

A married woman should not be desirous of attracting the eyes of any man but those of her husband.

He that allows himself to taste those pleasures which he denies his wife , acts like a man who would enjoin his wife to oppose those enemies to whom he has already surrendered.

E X A M P L E S.

Julius Sabinus , having engaged the interest of the Gauls , caused himself to be proclaimed emperor of Rome ; but being defeated , he fled to his country-house , and set it on fire , in order to raise a report that he had perished. This scheme answered his end , for he was there believed to have suffered a voluntary death. But , in the mean time , he lay concealed with his treasures (for he was immensely rich) in a cave , which he had caused to be dug in a solitary place , and which was known only to two of his freed-men , upon whose fidelity he could depend. He might easily have withdrawn into Germany ; but he could not prevail on himself to abandon his wife , whom he passionately loved. Sabinus , that no one might doubt of his death , did not , for some time , even undeceive his wife , who solemnized his exequies with great pomp , bewailed him with many tears , and, at last , no longer able to bear the loss of a a husband for whom she had the sincerest affection , resolved not to out-live him , and began to abstain from all food. This news alarmed Sabinus ; and therefore , by means of Martialis , one of his freed-men , he informed her that he was still alive , and acquainted her with the place where he lay concealed , desiring her at the same time to suppress her joy , lest the secret might thence be betrayed. Empona heard the relation with inexpressible pleasure ; and pretending business in the country , flew to her husband. The cave to her was then preferable to a palace , for there only she was

A 2

happy. She went frequently to see him , and sometimes contrived to stay whole weeks unsuspected. She had even two children by him , who were born and brought up in the cave. When at Rome , she continued to bewail him as dead , and concealed the whole with exemplary fidelity and wonderful address ; nay she found means to convey him into the city , upon what motive I know not ; and from thence back to his cave , so well disguised , that he was by no one known. But after he had passed nine years in this manner , he was, at length , discovered by some persons who narrowly watched his wife , upon her frequently absenting herself from her own house, and followed her to the cave without being discovered. Sabinus was immediately seized , and sent to Rome loaded with chains , together with his wife , who throwing herself at the emperor's feet , and presenting to him her two tender infants , endeavoured with her tears and entreaties to move him to compassion. Vespasian , the emperor , could not help weeping at so affecting an object ; nevertheless, he condemned both her and her husband , and caused them soon after to be executed.

TACIT. HIST. l. 4. c. 67. PLUT. AMAT.

Cyrus, king of Persia, had taken captive the young prince of Armenia, together with his beautiful and blooming princess, whom he had lately married, and of whom he was passionately fond. When both were brought to the tribunal, Cyrus asked the prince, what he would give to be re-instated in his kingdom? He answered, with an air of indifference, « That as for his crown, and his own liberty, he valued them at a very low rate. But if Cyrus would restore his beloved princess to her native dignity and hereditary possessions, he should infinitely rejoice, and would pay, (this he uttered with tenderness and ardor) would willingly pay his life for the purchase. » —— When all the prisoners were dismissed with freedom, it is impossible to be expressed how they were charmed with their royal benefactor; some celebrated his martial accomplishments; some applauded his social virtues, all were prodigal of their praise, and lavish in grateful acknowledgment. And you, said the prince, addressing himself to his bride, What think you of Cyrus, *I did not observe him,* said the princess. —— Not observe him! Upon what then was your attention fixed? Upon that *dear* and *generous* man, who declared,

A 3

« that he would purchase *my liberty* at the *expence* of *his own life.* »

What an idea of chastity! and at the same time , what a wonderful simplicity and delicacy of thought are here in the answer of the young princess , who had no eyes but for her husband !

XENOPH. DE CYRI INST. l. 3.

AFFECTION PARENTAL.

SENTIMENTS.

As the vexations which parents receive from their children hasten the approach of age , and double the force of years , so the comforts which they reap from them , are balm to all other sorrows , and disappoint the injuries of time. Parents repeat their lives in their offsprings , and their concern for them is so near , that they feel all their sufferings , and taste all their enjoyments, as much as if they regarded their own persons.

However strong we may suppose the fondness of a father for his children , yet they will find more lively marks of tenderness in the bosom of a mother. There are no ties in nature to compare with those which unite an affectionate mother to her children, when they repay her tenderness with obedience and love.

EXAMPLES.

Solon inquiring of Thales, the Milesian philosopher, Why, considering the happy situation of his affairs, he had neither wife nor children; Thales, for the present, made him no answer. A few days after he introduced a stranger, properly instructed, who said, that he came ten days ago from Athens. Solon immediately asked him what news he brought from thence : I know of nothing extraordinary, replied he, except that the whole city celebrated the funeral of a young man, the son of a citizen, most eminent for his virtues, who, it seems, went abroad upon his travels. Miserable man! cried Solon : but did not you hear his name? I did, returned the stranger, but I have forgot it; this I remember, that he was particularly famous for his wisdom and his justice. Was it Solon? said our philosopher : it was, answered the stranger. Upon this our legislator began to beat his head, to weep, and to discover all the symptoms of the

deepest sorrow. But Thales interposing,
with a smile, addressed him thus, « These,
O Solon, are things which make me afraid
of marriage and children, since these are capable of affecting even so wise a man as you;
be not, however, concerned, for this is all
a fiction. » Whether on this occasion, or
on the real loss of a son, is uncertain, Solon
being desired by a person not to weep, since
weeping would avail nothing : he answered with much humanity and good sense, *And
for this cause I weep.*

UNIV. HIST.

Cornelia the illustrious mother of the
Gracchi, after the death of her husband,
who left her twelve children, applied herself to the care of her family, with a wisdom
and prudence that acquired her universal
esteem. Only three out of the twelve lived
to years of maturity; one daugther, Sem-
pronia, whom she married to the second
Scipio Africanus; and two sons, Tiberius
and Caius, whom she brought up with so
much care; that, though they were generally acknowledged to have been born with
the most happy geniuses and dispositions,
it was judged that they were still more

indebted to education than nature. The answer she gave a Campanian lady concerning them is very famous , and includes in it great instructions for ladies and mothers.

That lady , who was very rich , and still fonder of pomp and shew , after having displayed in a visit she made her , her diamonds, pearls, and richest jewels, earnestly desired Cornelia to let her see her jewels also: Cornelia dexterously turned the conversation to another subject , to wait the return of her sons , who were gone to the public schools. When they returned, and entered their mother's apartment , she said to the Campanian lady, pointing to them with her hand, *These are my jewels , and the only ornaments I admire.* And such ornaments , which are the strength and support of society, add a brighter lustre to the fair than all the jewels of the East.

AFFECTION FILIAL.
SENTIMENTS.

IT may be truly said , that if persons are undutiful to their parents, they seldom prove good to any other relation.

The honour which children are required
to give to their father and mother, includes
in it, love, reverence, obedience, and relief. It is usual with Providence to retaliate
men's disobedience to their parents in kind:
commonly our own children shall pay us
home for it.

Where shall we find the person who hath
received from any one benefits so great, or
so many, as children from their parents ?
To them it is they owe their very existence,
and consequently all the pleasures and enjoyments of life.

No one will expect a return of kindness,
however considerable, from him who can
shew himself unmindful of what he oweth
his parents.

To see a father treating his sons like an
elder brother, and to see sons covet their
father's company and conversation, because
they think him the wisest and most agreeable man of their acquaintance, is the most
amiable picture the eye can behold; it is a
transplanted self-love, as sacred as friendship, as pleasurable as love, and as happy
as religion can make it.

If every father remembered his own
thoughts and inclinations when he was a

son , and every son remembered what he expected from his father , when he himself was in a state of dependency; this one reflection would keep fathers from being rigid , or sons dissolute.

E X A M P L E S.

T. Manlius , the Roman dictator , having exercised great violence and cruelty over the citizens , was cited at the expiration of his office to answer for his conduct. Among other things that were laid to his charge , he was accused of treating with barbarity one of his own sons. Manlius , it seems , had no other cause of complaint against this son than his having an impediment in his speech. For this reason he was banished far from the city , from his home , and the company of those of his own age and fortune , and condemned to servile works , and a prison like a slave. All were highly exasperated against so severe a dictator , and so inhuman a father , except the son himself , who moved with filial piety , and under the greatest concern that he should furnish matter of accusation against his father , resolved upon a most extraordinary method to relieve him. One morning , without apprising any body ,

he came to the city armed with a dagger,
and went directly to the house of the tribune
Pomponius, who had accused his father.
Pomponius was yet in bed. He sent up his
name, and was immediately admitted by
the tribune, who did not doubt but he was
come to discover to him some new instances
of his father's severity. After they had saluted each other, young Manlius desired a private conference; and as soon as he saw himself alone with the tribune, he drew out his
dagger, presented it to his breast, and declared he would stab him that moment, if
he did not swear in the form he should dictate, « Never to hold the assembly of the
people for accusing his father ». Pomponius,
who saw the dagger glittering at his breast,
himself alone without arms, and attacked by
a robust young man, full of a bold confidence in his own strength, took the oath
demanded of him, and afterwards confessed
with a kind of complacency in the thing,
and a sincerity which sufficiently argued he
was not sorry for what he had done, that
it was that violence which obliged him to
desist from his enterprise.

Liv. l. 7. ch. 4, 5.

Demetrius,

Demetrius , king of Macedon , being imprisoned by Seleucus , he wrote a letter to his son Antigonus , commending to him the care of his concerns in Greece ; exhorting him to govern his subjects justly, to act always with moderation , and to look upon him , (his father) as dead ; conjuring him never to part with any of his cities , or give up any thing to Seleucus to procure his liberty. But notwithstanding this letter might in the opinion of the world have freed him from all censure ; yet he immediately offered Seleucus not only all that he held in Greece , but his own person in hostage for his father's liberty. But this was refused. However , Antigonus continued earnestly to solicit it , by the most pressing and passionate importunities and offers as long as Demetrius lived ; going in deep mourning during that space (three years) and never once partaking of any feasts or diversions while his father was in prison. As soon as he heard of his death , and that his ashes were coming from Syria , he sailed with a noble fleet to the Archipelago to meet them. He then deposited them in a golden urn, which, when he entered the harbour of Corinth , he placed in the poop of the royal galley , set his crown upon it , and

B

covered it with a canopy of purple, himself standing by clothed in deep mourning, and his eyes red with tears.

It is worth observing, that Demetrius likewise had rendered himself very remarkable for his filial piety : for we are told by Plutarch, Justin, and others, that Demetrius was not only dutiful and loyal to his father, but had so warm an affection for his person, that he was, in the strictest sense of the words, his father's best friend. As all degrees of bliss are either heightened or lessened by comparison, so the happiness of Antigonus (the father of Demetrius) in this respect, appeared with the brighter lustre on account of the family-dissensions in the courts of his several rivals. Of this he was so sensible, that having given audience one day to the ambassadors of Cassander, Ptolemy, and Lysimachus, and they being withdrawn, he ordered them to be called back, because his son Demetrius, coming in warm from hunting, went into his father's apartment, saluted him, and then sat down with his javelin in his hand. When the ambassadors demanded what his pleasure was, «Tell your masters, says Antigonus, besides what I before mentioned, upon what terms my son and I live ».

The sense the father had of his son's inviolable attachment to him, made him so readily compliment him with the regal dignity, giving him not only a share in the government, but the *title* of king; and he never had any occasion to repent of his confidence.

JUST. l. 16. PLUT. IN DEMET. COR. NEP. DE REG. c. 3.

While Octavius was at Samos, after the famous battle of Actium, which made him master of the universe, he held a council to examine the prisoners which had been engaged in Antony's party. Among the rest there was brought before him an old man named Metellus, oppressed with years and infirmities, disfigured with a long beard and a neglected head of hair, but especially by his clothes, which by his ill fortune were become very ragged. The son of this Metellus was one of the judges, and he had great difficulty of knowing his father in the deplorable condition in which he saw him. At last, however, having recollected his features, instead of being ashamed to own

B 2

him, he ran to embrace him, crying bitterly. Afterwards, turning towards the tribunal, « Cæsar, says he, my father has been your enemy, and I your officer : he deserves to be punished, and I to be rewarded. The favour I desire of you is either to save him on my account, or to order me to be put to death with him. » All the judges were touched with compassion at this affecting scene ; Octavius himself relented, and granted to old Metellus his life and liberty.

APPIAN.

Epaminondas, without all doubt, was one of the greatest generals, and one of the best men which Greece ever produced. Before him the city of Thebes was not distinguished by any memorable action, and after him it was not famous for its virtues, but its misfortunes, till it sunk into its original obscurity; so that it saw its glory take birth and expire with this great man. The victory he obtained at Leuctra had drawn the eyes and admiration of all the neighbouring people upon Epaminondas, who looked upon him as the support of Thebes, as the triumphant conqueror of all Sparta, as the deliverer of all Greece; in a word, as the greatest man , and the most excellent captain that ever was in the world. In the midst of this universal applause , so capable of making the general of an army forget the man for the victor , Epaminondas , little sensible to so affecting and so deserved a glory , *My joy* , said he , *arises from my sense of that which the news of my victory will give my father and my mother.*

PLUT. IN CORIOL. p. 215.

AFFECTION FRATERNAL.

SENTIMENTS.

THOUGH all mankind spring from the same head , and are bound to cultivate a mutual good-will to each other ; yet this duty is not so obvious and striking as that which is incumbent on those who belong to the same family.

Nothing can approach nearer to self-love than fraternal affection : and there is but a short remove from our own concern and happiness to theirs who come from the same stock , and are partakers of the same blood Nothing , therefore , can be more horrible

B 3

than discord and animosity among members so allied ; and nothing so beautiful as harmony and love.

This relation is formed by nature , not by choice ; and tho' it has many things in common with , yet it is prior to the obligations of friendship : consequently nature and reason dictate that there should be a peculiar affection between brethren. We are not obliged , however, to make a brother or sister an intimate or bosom friend in preference to one who is not akin. Diversity of temper , and want of suitable qualifications may render it unsafe and improper. But where friendship and fraternity meet in the same persons , such a conjunction adds a lustre to the relation.

Among brethren an hearty love of benevolence , an ardent concern of each other's welfare , a readiness to serve and promote it , are the peculiar offices of this relation ; and though friends are to have their share , yet the claim of kindred is first and ordinarily strongest.

EXAMPLES.

Darius , king of Persia , had three sons by his first wife , the daughter of Gabrias , all three born before their father came to the crown ; and four more by Atossa , the daughter of Cyrus , who were all born after their father's accession to the throne. Artabazanes, called by Justin, Artimenes, was the eldest of the former , and Xerxes of the latter. Artabazanes alledged , in his own behalf , that the right of succession , according to the custom and practice of all nations , belonged to him preferably to all the rest. Xerxes's argument for succeeding his father was , that as he was the son of Atossa , the daughter of Cyrus , who founded the Persian empire, it was more just that the crown of Cyrus should devolve upon one of his descendants , than upon one that was not. Demaratus , a Spartan king , at that time at the court of Persia , secretly suggested to Xerxes another argument to support his pretensions ; that Artabazanes was indeed the eldest son of Darius ; but he , Xerxes , was the eldest son of the king ; and therefore Artabazanes being born when his father was but a private person , all he could pretend to , on account of his seniority , was only to inherit his private estate ; but that he , Xerxes, being the first-born son of the king , had the best right to succeed to the

crown. He further supported this argument
by the example of the Lacedemonians , who.
admitted none to inherit the kingdom , but
those children that were born after their father's accession. The right of succession was
accordingly determined in favour of Xerxes.
Both Justin and Plutarch take notice of the
prudent conduct of these two brothers on so
nice an occasion. According to their manner
of relating this fact , Artabazanes was absent when the king died ; and Xerxes immediately assumed all the marks , and exercised all the functions of the sovereignty.
But upon his brother's returning home , he
quitted the diadem , and the tiara , which
he wore in such a manner as only suited the
king , went out to meet him , and shewed
him all imaginable respect. They agreed to
make their uncle Artabanes the arbitrator of
their difference ; and without any further ap-
peal , to acquiesce in his decision.

All the while this dispute lasted , the two
brothers shewed one another all the demon-
strations of a truly fraternal affection , by
keeping up a continual intercourse of presents
and entertainments : whence their mutual
esteem and confidence for each other banished all fears and suspicions on both sides , and

introduced an unconstrained cheerfulness, and a perfect security.

This is a spectacle, says Justin, highly worthy of our admiration : to see whilst most brothers are at daggers–drawing with one another about a small patrimony, with what moderation and temper both waited for a decision, which was to dispose of the greatest empire then in the universe. When Artabanes gave judgment in favour of Xerxes, Artabazanes the same instant prostrated himself before him, acknowledging him for his master, and placed him upon the throne with his own hand ; by which proceeding he shewed a greatness of soul truly royal, and infinitely superior to all human dignities. This ready acquiescence in a sentence so contrary to his interest, was not the effect of an artful policy, that knows how to dissemble upon occasion, and to receive honour to itself from what it could not prevent : no ; it proceeded from a real respect for the laws, a sincere affection for his brother, and an indifference for that which so warmly inflames the ambition of mankind, and so frequently arms the nearest relations against each other. For his part, during his whole life, he continued firmly attached to the interests of Xerxes, and prosecuted them with so much ardor and zeal, that he lost his life in his service at the battle of Salamin.

PLUT. DE FRAT. AMORE . p. 144. JUST. l. 2. c. 10.

The Chinese have been remarkable for the purity of their morals, the simplicity of their manners, and the cultivation of the social virtues. The examples of their rulers and great men have very much contributed to confirm the people in the practice of moral duties ; for, perhaps, few princes ever exhibited greater instances of an amiable and virtuous conduct. Cemcu, who was a disciple of and commentator upon their celebrated philosopher Confusius, gives us the following instances of brotherly affection :

The king of Cucho had three sons, and like many other parents, having most affection for the youngest, some days before his death declared him his successor, to the exclusion of his brethren. This proceeding was the more extraordinary, as it was contrary to the laws of the kingdom. The people, therefore, thought that after the death of the king, they might without any crime raise the eldest son to the throne. This design was universally approved of : but the new king calling to mind his father's last words , rejected the offer, and taking the crown, placed it on the head of his youngest brother , publicly declaring that he renounced it , and thought himself unworthy of *it* , *as he was* excluded *by his father's will* ; and his father could not now retract what he had done. His brother , being affected with such a generous action , instantly intreated him not to oppose the inclination of the people , who desired him for their ruler. He urged , that he alone was the lawful successor to the crown which he refused, and that their father could not infringe the laws of the kingdom ; that he had been betrayed by an extravagant fondness ; and that , *in a word* , the people had the power of redressing any breach in the established law. Nothing, however, was capable of persuading his brother to accept of the crown. There was a glorious contest between the two princes ; and as they perceived that the dispute would be endless , they retired from court : thus each having both conquered and been vanquished , they went to end their days together in peaceful solitude , and left the kingdom to their other brother.

AMBITION.

SENTIMENTS.

AMBITION to rule is more vehement than malice to revenge. It must be confessed, that no passion has produced more dreadful effects than ambition ; and yet , methinks , ambition is not a vice but in a vicious mind. In a virtuous mind it is a virtue , and will be found to take its colour from the character in which it is mixed.

— Ambition is at distance
A goodly prospect , tempting to the view :
The height delights us , and the mountain top
Looks beautiful , because 'tis nigh to heaven ;
But we n'er look how sandy's the foundation ,
What storms will batter, and what tempests shake us!
When wild ambition in the heart we find ,
Farewel content and quiet of the mind :
For glittering clouds we leave the solid shore,
And wonted happiness returns no more.
Ambition is the dropsy of the soul ,
Whose thirst we must not yield to but controul.
Be prudent , and the shore in prospect keep ,
In a weak boat trust not the deep :]
Plac'd beneath envy , above envying rise;
Pity great men , great things despise.

EXAMPLES

E X A M P L E S.

M. Manlius was a patrician of one of the most illustrious houses in Rome. He had been consul , and had acquired very great reputation by many glorious exploits , and in particular by the signal service he had done his country in saving the Capitol, when upon the point of being taken by the Gauls ; but a secret vanity and ambition , which Manlius suffered to take root in his heart , corrupted all his great qualities , and entirely sullied his glory. As he did not believe himself so much considered by the senators as he deserved , he threw himself into a party of the people , and entered into a strict union with the tribunes. He spoke contemptuously of the senators , and flattered the multitude. In a word , he chose rather to have a great than a good reputation : nothing would satisfy him but the supreme authority. The measures , however, which he employed to accomplish his design were so ill concerted , that Manlius was cited before the dictator to answer for his conduct. He had the rashness to say , in the assemblies which he held in his own house , that the senators had appropriated the gold intended for the payment of

C

the auxiliary troops to their own use ; and
had concealed great treasures which belonged to the public. Manlius was ordered to
make good his charge ; which not being able
to do , he vas committed to prison as a seditious person and a false accuser. Seeing himself seized by the dictator's officer, he omitted
nothing to make the people rise in his defence. He invoked all the gods , that inha-
bited the Capitol , imploring them to aid
him , who had so courageously defended
them. « How ! said he , « shall the hand that
has preserved your temples from the fury of
the Gauls be disgraced with vile chains ? »
The whole people were penetrated with the
most lively affliction. Multitudes passed not
only the day , but even the night , round the
prison ; and menaced to break down the
gates. The senate chose to grant them that ,
of their own accord , which they were upon
the point of taking by force ; and caused
Manlius to be set at liberty. But by that timorous policy , instead of appeasing the se-
dition , they only gave it an head. Manlius ,
released from prison , grew more violent ,
and less cautious : in short, his design to
overturn the government , and enslave the
people was so evident that he was again seized

and imprisoned. He now began to lose all hopes, and the people's eyes were fully opened; they saw they had been deceived. As for Manlius, when he came to take his trial, he appeared in a mourning habit; but without a single senator, relation, friend, or even his own brothers along with him, to express concern ⬤r his fate. So much did the love of liberty, and the fear of being enslaved, prevail in the hearts of the Romans over all the ties of blood and nature! After a fair hearing, he was condemned to be thrown from the top of the Capitol; and the same place which had been the theatre of his glory, became that of his shame and infamy.

Such was the end of a man who might have been the ornament of his country, if he had not been born in a free state. We here see how many glorious and excellent qualities, the lust of reigning rendered not only fruitless, but odious and detestable.

Liv. l. iv. 12.

Marius, so famous in the Roman history, was a man that had but one passion, the desire of aggrandizing himself, to which he never made any scruple to sacrifice every thing: for he never knew either integrity,

C 2

sincerity, or gratitude, when the pursuit of
his views were in question. It was this ambition that made him quit the plough and take
up the profession of arms, by which he was
in hopes of making his fortune. He succeeded
beyond all expectations: but after having passed through every honour in the Roman government; having acquired a considerable
fortune, and made a good alliance, by mar-
rying Julia, Cæsar's aunt; instead of being
satisfied with his uncommon success, and
enjoying the fruits of his toils and dangers,
at the age of seventy, when he was become
exceedingly gross and heavy, and oppressed
with many infirmities, he was determined
to take on him the war against Mithridates,
king of Pontus. He imagined, that this war
furnished an occasion of acquiring great
glory and riches, without much danger. But
Sylla, as consul, was general of the Roman
armies; and had a just right to appropriate
the first and most glorious province to himself: he was likewise appointed to this command by the senate. Marius opposed him.
The contest ran high: and a civil war ensued. Sylla besieges the city of Rome, and
Marius is obliged to save himself by flight.
Sylla makes an alteration in the government,

and an order is issued out in all the cities of
Italy, to seize and kill Marius wherever he
should be found. After wandering from place
to place, and suffering a variety of difficulties, dangers and distresses, both by sea
and land, he is at last treacherously set on
shore in the province of an enemy, without aid,
without defence, and abandoned by all the
world. He, however, did not abandon himself; but crossing marshes, ditches full of
water, and muddy grounds, he came at
length to a poor wood-cleaver's cottage. He
threw himself at his feet, and conjured him to
save a man, who, if he escaped danger,
would reward him beyond his hopes. The
peasant, whether he knew him, or was
struck with the loftiness and majesty of his
appearance, which his misfortunes had not
effaced, answered, « That if he only wanted
rest, he might find it in his cottage; but if he
fled from enemies, he would shew him a
safer retreat ». Marius having accepted the
last offer, the man conducted him to a hollow
place, near a marsh, where he covered him
with leaves, reeds, and rushes. Marius had
scarce entered this dismal retreat, before he
heard his enemies in pursuit of him. They
questioned, pressed, and menaced the wood-

man, for concealing an enemy of the public, condemned to die by the Roman senate. Marius had no resource left : he quitted his retreat, undressed himself, and plunged into the black and muddy water of the marsh. This dirty asylum could not conceal him. His pursuers ran to him ; and having drawn him out of the water naked, and all covered with mud, they put a cord about his neck, and dragged him to Minturnæ, where they delivered him to the magistrates.

May I be allowed here to desire the reader to consider Marius attentively in his deplorable state at this moment ? What might then be his thoughts ! How much ought he to have abhorred a fatal ambition that, from the height of greatness and glory, had plunged him into an abyss of misery below the condition of mankind ! And what a lesson is this to those who are never contented with their condition ; and who imagine they want all things, when but a single object is wanting to their insatiable avidity !

But such are the vissicitudes of human life, that even when hope forsook him, and while the hand was lifted up, he escaped the blow. From the lowest state of misery, he yet rose to the pinnacle of what is falfely called honour and greatness. By the intrigues of a faction, he returned to Rome; where he gave the most melancholy proofs that his misfortunes had neither made him wiser nor better, had neither taught him humility, compassion, nor moderation. Being at first, as it were, only protected by Cinna, who was then master of Rome, he affected an air of dejection; but his unextinguished ambition soon rendered him the soul of the party. Having now the sword in his hand, and burning with revenge, and indignation he cut down all before him: naturally merciless and cruel, he spared neither age, dignity, nor virtue; a look, a nod, determined at once the fate of the most illustrious persons; every one whom he in the least suspected or disliked were put to death, without the least form or ceremony. The slaughter, attended with plundering of houses, and the most criminal violences, continued five days and five nights in Rome, which became one general scene of horror; unpitied shrieks and cries were every where heard, the canals poured down with human blood, while the lifeless bodies, even of the most eminent senators, were trampled under foot; for it was prohibited to give them burial. These were the glorious fruits of ambition ! By these without doubt, Marius intended to render himself great and happy; but he found it quite otherwise. The state of prosperity in which he was, did not calm the disquiets occasioned by the fear of Sylla's return, who was carrying on the war with Mithridates. So formidable an avenger made Marius tremble and he could not even dissemble his fears. These thoughts tormented him continually, and occasioned his nights to pass without sleep, which began to affect his health and spirits. He therefore abandoned himself to the excesses of the table ; and to spend his nights in drinking with his friends and dependants. By this regimen he soon inflamed his blood. He was attacked with a fever, which presently seized his head; and, in his delirium, he raved of nothing but the war with Mithridates: he imagined he had the command of it; and not only spoke, but made gestures, and assumed the attitude of a man that fights, or of a general giving orders : so violent and incurable was the passion, and so deeply had it taken root in his heart, with which ambition and jealousy uniting, had inspired him for that command. Thus, says Plutarch, at the age of seventy, the only man who had been seven times consul, and possessing riches that might have sufficed for several kings, lamented as one suffering indigence, and died before he could put his views in execution. Wretch! that instead of enjoying the gifts of fortune with gratitude, suffered himself to be deprived of the present in being wholly engrossed by a chimerical future. And yet Marius was one of the most famous Romans. But surely when Marius, or Alexander the Great, Julius Cæsar, or in modern times, Lewis XIV. are treated as great men, or as heroes, it holds forth the most flagrant example of the weakness of mankind who so little understand their interests, as to annex the idea of greatness and heroism to the fatal art of destroying their species; and who can admit, that such heroism can subsist with vices most pernicious to society.

His fortune seems scarcely more worthy of envy, than his conduct of praise. For if, instead of suffering ourselves to be dazzled by the vain splendor of riches and dignity, we consider what it cost him to acquire and secure the possession of them; what intrigues, cabals, anxieties! add to these, the torments of envy, fears, vexation, on being often forced to give way, and lastly, the deplorable circumstances of his flight; would he not have been more happy, if, tranquil in the obscure state he was born, cultivating the little land either left him by his father, or acquired by himself, he had led a life exempt from care and dangers.

To the foregoing examples I will only add that of Rome itself, of which Marius was both the preserver and executioner. What a dreadful situation was she in amidst all her prosperity and greatness! She is victorious over all her enemies, and tyrannized over by her own citizens. She puts to flight and cuts to pieces foreign armies, and is drowned in her own blood. Ambition prompts her to give laws to all nations; at the same time she cannot support her own, which change every instant with the caprice of the tyrants that oppress her: and it is even this prosperity that gives birth to all her calamities. Modest and happy as long as she was weak and low; it is good fortune that introduces the most horrid of vices and calamities into her bosom. Such is the error and uncertainty of human things! So ignorant are men of what constitutes their real happiness! Let us conclude then, that there is no solid felicity, either for states or private persons, but in the practice of virtue; and that virtue is much more the friend and companion of mediocrity, than of too great an} elevation of fortune.

B E N E F I C E N C E.

S E N T I M E N T S.

M A N is naturally a beneficent creature. The greatest pleasure wealth can afford is that of doing good. All men of estates are in effect but trustees for the benefit of the distressed; and will be so reckoned when they are to give an account.

Defer not charities till death. He that doth so, is rather liberal of another man's substance than of his own.

Men of the noblest dispositions think themselves happiest when others share with them in their happiness.

No object is more pleasing to the eye than the sight of a man whom you have obliged; nor any music so agreeable to the ear as the

voice of one that owns you for his benefactor.

It is better to be of the number of those
who need relief, than of those who want
hearts to give it.

When we would exercise this virtue,
we ought to deliberate with ourselves
whether our circumstances will answer
out intended bounty; for there are some
who are generous to strangers, to the prejudice of themselves, their friends, and relations.

We ought to consult the worth of the
person whom we have chosen for the
object of our liberality. The wicked, debauched, and extravagant, are neither en-
titled to pity nor relief: but the cry of virtue
in distress ought to be irresistible.

That which is given with pride and
ostentation, is rather an ambition than a
bounty. Let a benefit be ever so considerable, the manner of conferring it is the
noblest part.

E X A M P L E S.

When the province of Azazene was ravaged by the Romans, seven thousand Persians

sians were brought prisoners to the city of Amida, where they fell into extreme want. Acases, bishop of that place, having assembled his clergy, represented to them, in the most pathetic terms, the misery of those unhappy prisoners. He then observed, that as the Almighty preferred mercy to sacrifice, he would certainly be better pleased with the relief of these his creatures, than with being served with gold and silver vessels in their churches. The clergy entertained this notion, not only with readiness, but with applause; sold all the consecrated vessels; and having maintained the Persians during the war, sent the seven thousand home at the conclusion of the peace, with money in their pockets. Varenes, the Persian monarch, was so charmed with this action, that he sent to invite the bishop to his capital, where he received him with the utmost reverence, and did the Christians many favours at his request.

SOCRAT. HIST. ECCLES. lib. vii. c. 7.

About the year A. M. 3782, the island of Rhodes suffered very great damages by an earthquake: the walls of the city, with the

D

arsenals, and the narrow passes in the havens, where the ships of that island were laid up, were reduced to a very ruinous condition; and the famous Colossus, which was esteemed one of the wonders of the world, was thrown down and entirely destroyed. It is natural to think that this earthquake spared neither private nor public structures, nor even the temples of the gods. The loss sustained by it amounted to immense sums; and the Rhodians, reduced to the utmost distress, sent deputations to all the neighbouring princes to implore their relief in that melancholy conjuncture. An emulation worthy of praise, and not to be paralleled in history, prevailed in favour of that deplorable city: and Hiero and Gelon in Sicily, and Ptolemy in Egypt signalized themselves in a peculiar manner on that occasion. The two former of these princes contributed above an hundred talents, and erected two statues in the public place; one of which represented the people of Rhodes, and the other those of Syracuse, the former was crowned by the latter, to testify, as Polybius observes, that the Syracusians

thought the opportunity of relieving the
Rhodians a favour and obligation to themselves. Ptolemy, besides his other expences,
which amounted to a very considerable
sum, supplied that people with 300 talents,
100,000 bushels of corn, and a sufficient
quantity of timber for building ten galleys
of ten benches of oars, and as many more
of three benches, besides an infinite quantity of wood for other buildings; all which
donations were accompanied with three
thousand talents, for erecting the Colossus
anew. Antigonus, Seleucus, Prusias, Mithridates, and all the princes, as well as
cities, signalized their liberality on the occasion. Even private persons emulated each
other in sharing in this glorious act of humanity; and historians have recorded that
a lady, whose name was Chryseis, furnished, from her own substance, an hundred thousand bushels of corn. Rhodes,
in consequence of these liberalities, was
re-established in a more opulent and splendid
state than she had ever experienced before,
if we only except the Colossus.

PObYB. L. 5. p. 428.

D 2

CLEMENCY.

SENTIMENTS.

CLEMENCY is not only the privilege, the honour, and the duty of a prince, but it is also his security, and better than all garrisons, forts, and guards, to preserve himself and his dominions in safety. It is the brightest jewel in a monarch's crown.

As meekness moderates anger, so clemency moderates punishment.

That prince is truly royal who masters himself; looks upon all injuries as below him; and governs by equity and reason, not by passion.

Clemency is profitable for all; does well in private persons, but is much more beneficial in princes.

Mischiefs contemned, lose their force.

EXAMPLES.

Deucetius, according to Diodorus, was chief over the people who were properly called Sicilians. Having united them all into one body, he became very powerful, and formed several great enterprizes.

It was he who built the city Palica, near the temple of the gods, called Palici. This city was famous on account of some wonders which are related of it; and still more for the sacred nature of the oaths which were there taken, the violation whereof was said to be always followed by a sudden and exemplary punishment. This was a secure asylum for all persons who were oppressed by superior power; and especially for slaves who were unjustly abused or cruelly treated by their masters. They continued in safety in this temple, till certain arbiters and mediators had made their peace; and there was not a single instance of a master's having ever forfeited the promise he had made to pardon his slaves.

This Deucetius, after having been successful on a great many occasions, and gained several victories, particulary over the Syracusians, saw his fortune change on a sudden by the loss of a battle, and was abandoned by the greatest part of his forces. In the consternation and despondency into which so general and sudden a def

sertion threw him, he formed such a resolution as despair only could suggest. He
withdrew in the night to Syracuse, advanced as far as the great square in the
city, and there falling prostrate at the foot
of the altar, he abandoned his life and
dominions to the mercy of the Syracusians;
that is, to his professed enemies. The sin-
gularity of this spectacle drew great numbers
of people to it. The magistrates immediately convened the people, and debated on the
affair. They first heard the orators, whose
business was generally to address the people
by their speeches; and these animated them
prodigiously against Deucetius, as a public
enemy whom Providence seemed to throw
in their way, to revenge and punish, by
his death, all the injuries he had done the
republic. A speech in this stile struck all the
virtuous part of the assembly with horror.
The most ancient and the wisest of the senators represented, « That they were not to
consider what punishment Deucetius deserved; but how it behoved the Syracusians to
behave on that occasion: that they ought
not to look upon him any longer as an enemy,
but as a suppliant, a character by which
his person became sacred and inviolable.

There was a goddess (Nemesis) who took vengeance of crimes , especially of cruelty and impiety ; and who doubtless , would not suffer that to go unpunished; that besides the baseness and inhumanity there is in insulting the unfortunate , and in crushing those who are already under one's foot , it was worthy the grandeur and goodness natural to the Syracusians , to exert their clemency even to those who least deserved it »

All the people came into this opinion , and with one consent spared Deucetius's life. He was ordered to reside in Corinth : and the Syracusians engaged to furnish Deucetius with all things necessary for his subsisting honourably there. What reader , who compares these two different opinions , does not perceive which of them was the noblest and most generous !.

DIOD. p. 67 — 70.

The Athenians having made war upon the Syracusians , the army of the former , under the command of Nicias and Demosthenes , was totally defeated ; and the generals obliged to surrender at discretion. The victors , having entered their capital in triumph, the next day a council was held to deliberate what was to be done with the prisoners. Diocles, one of the leaders of the greatest authority among the people, proposed, that all the Athenians who were born of free parents, and all such Sicilians as had joined with them, should be imprisoned, and be maintained on bread and water only; that the slaves, and all the Atticks should be publicly sold; and that the two Athenian generals should be first scourged with rods, and then put to death. This last article exceedingly disgusted all wise and compassionate Syracusians. Hermocrates, who was very famous for his probity and justice, attempted to make some remonstrances to the people; but they would not hear him : and the shouts which echoed from all sides prevented him from continuing his speech. At that instant, an ancient man, venerable for his great age and gravity, who in this war had lost two sons, the only heirs to his name and estate, made his servants carry him to the tribunal for harangues; and, the instant he appeared, a profound silence was made.

« You here behold, says he, an unfortunate father, who has felt more than any other Syracusian the fatal effects of this war, by the death of two sons, who formed all the consolation, and were the only supports of my old age. I cannot, indeed, forbear admiring their courage and felicity in sacrificing to their country's welfare a life which they would one day have been deprived of by the common course of nature; but then, I cannot but be sensibly affected with the cruel wound which their death hath made in my heart; nor forbear hating and despising the Athenians, the authors of this unhappy war, as the murderers of my children. But however, I cannot conceal one circumstance, which is, that I am less sensible for my private afflictions, than for the honour of my country; and I see it exposed to eternal infamy, by the barbarous advice which is now given you. The Athenians, indeed, merit the worst kind of treatment that could be inflicted on them, for so unjustly declaring war against us : but have not the gods, the just avengers of crimes, punished them, and avenged us sufficiently? When their generals laid down their arms, and surrendered, did not they do this in hopes of having their lives spared ? And if we put them to death, will it be possible for us to avoid the just reproach of our having violated the law of nations, and dishonoured our victory by unheard - of cruelty! What, will you suffer your glory to be thus sullied in the face of the whole world; and have it said, that a nation who first dedicated a temple to Clemency, had not found any in yours? Surely, victories and triumphs do not give immortal glory to a city : but the exercising mercy towards a vanquished enemy, the using moderation in the greatest prosperity, and the fearing to offend the gods, by a haughty and insolent pride. You doubtless have not forgotten that this Nicias, whose fate you are going to pronounce, was the very man who pleaded your cause in the assembly of the Athenians ; and who employed all his credit, and the whole power of his eloquence, to dissuade his country from embarking in this war. Should you, therefore, pronounce sentence of death on this worthy general, would it be a just reward for the zeal he shewed for your interest? With regard to myself, death would be less grievous to me, than the sight of so horrid an injustice committed by my countrymen and fellow-citizens. »

DIOD. l. 13. p. 149.

COMPASSION.

SENTIMENTS.

COMPASSION is the sense of our own misfortunes in those of another man. It is a wise foresight of the disasters that may befall us; which induces us to assist others, in order to engage them to return it on like occasions : so that the services we do the unfortunate are in reality so many anticipated kindnesses to ourselves.

Compassion proper to mankind appears;
Which nature witness'd when she lent us tears,
To shew by pitying looks, and melting eyes,
How with a suffering friend we sympathize.
Who can all sense of other's ills escape,
Is but a brute, at best, in human shape.

EXAMPLES.

It was a custom with Alexander the great to oblige the captive women whom he carried along with him to sing songs after the manner of their country. He happened among these women to perceive one who appeared in deeper affliction than the rest ; and who by a modest , and at the same time a noble confusion , discovered a greater reluctance than the others to appear in public. She was a perfect beauty ; which was very much heightened by her bashfulness , whilst she threw her eyes on the ground , and did all she could to conceal her face. The king soon imagined, by her air and mien , that she was not of vulgar birth ; and enquiring into it, the lady answered, that she was grand-daughter to Octius , who not long before had swayed the Persian sceptre , and daughter of his son ; that she had married Hystaspes , who was related to Darius , and general of a great army. Alexander being touched with compassion , when he heard the unhappy fate of a princess of the royal blood, and the sad condition to which she was reduced , not only gave her her liberty , but returned all her possessions ; and caused her husband to be sought for , in order that she might be restored to him.

Q. CURT. l. vi. c. 6.

As

As Alexander drew near the city of Persepolis, he perceived a large body of men, who exhibited a memorable example of the greatest misery. These were about four thousand Greeks, very far advanced in years; who having been made prisoners of war, had suffered all the torments which the Persian tyranny could inflict. The hands of some had been cut off, the feet of others, and others again had lost their noses and ears; after which the Persians having impressed by fire, barbarous characters on their faces, had the inhumanity to keep them as so many laughing-stocks, with which they sported perpetually. They appeared like so many shadows rather than men; speech being almost the only thing by which they were known to be such. Alexander could not refrain from tears at this sight; and as they unanimously besought him to commiserate their condition, he bid them with the utmost tenderness, not to despond; and assured them, that they should again see their wives and native country. This proposal, which one might suppose should naturally, have filled them with joy seemed to heighten their misery; and, with tears in their eyes, « How will it be possible », said some of

E

them, « for us to appear publicly before all
» Greece, in the dreadful condition to which
» we are reduced : a condition still more
» shameful than dissatisfactory ? The best
» way to bear misery is to conceal it ; and
» no country is so sweet to the wretched as
» solitude, and an oblivion of their past mis—
» fortunes ». They therefore besought the
king to permit them to continue in a country
where they had spent so many years ; and
to end their days among those who were
already accustomed to their misfortunes.
Alexander granted their request ; and presented each of them three thousand drachmas,
five men's suits of clothes, the same num—
ber of women's, two couple of oxen to
plough their lands, and corn to sow them :
he commanded the governor of the province
not to suffer them to be molested in any
manner, and ordered that they should be
free from taxes and tributes of every kind.
Such behaviour as this was truly royal.
Thrice happy those princes who are affected
with the pleasure which arises from the
doing of good actions, and who melt with
pity for the unfortunate !

Q. CURT.

CONSCIENCE.

SENTIMENTS.

MOST men are afraid of a bad name; but few fear their consciences.

The severest punishment of an injury is the consciousness of having done it; and no man suffers more than he that is turned over to the pain of repentance.

It costs us more to be miserable than would make us perfectly happy; how cheap and easy is the service of virtue; and how dear do we pay for our vices!

If a man cannot find ease within himself, it is to little purpose to seek it any where else.

EXAMPLES.

The caliph Montaser having caused his father to be put to death; some time after, looking over the rich furniture in the palace, and causing several pieces of tapestry to be opened before him, that he might examine them the more exactly; among the rest, he met with one which had in it the figure of

E 2

a very beautiful young man , mounted on a Persian horse , with a diadem on his head , and a circle of Persian characters round himself and his horse. The caliph, charmed with the beauty of the tapestry , sent for a Persian who understood the ancient Persic , and desired him to explain that inscription. The man read it , changed colour , and , after some hesitation , told the caliph , it was a Persic song , that had nothing in it worth hearing. The prince , however , would not be put off : he readily perceived there was something in it extraordinary : and therefore he commanded the interpreter to give him the true sense thereof immediately , as he valued his own safety. The man then told him , that the inscription ran thus : *I am Siroes , the son of Chosroes , who slew my father to gain his crown , which I kept but six months.* This affected the caliph Montaser so much , that he died in two or three days , when he had reigned about the same space of time. This story is perfectly well attested.

UNIV. HIST. vol. xi. p. 197.

A Jeweller , a man of a good character , and considerable wealth , having occasion

In the way of his business to travel at some
distance from the place of his abode , took
along with him a servant , in order to take
care of his portmanteau. He had with him
some of his best jewels , and a large sum of
money , to which his servant was likewise
privy. The master having occasion to dis-
mount on the road , the servant watching
his opportunity , took a pistol from his
master's saddle , and shot him dead on
the spot : then rifled him of his jewels and
money , and hanging a large stone to his
neck , he threw him into the nearest canal.
With this booty he made off to a distant
part of the country , where he had reason to
believe that neither he nor his master were
known. There he began to trade in a very
low way at first , that his obscurity might
screen him from observation , and in the
course of a good many years , seemed to rise
by the natural progress of business , into
wealth and consideration : so that his good
fortune appeared at once the effect and reward of industry and virtue. Of these he
counterfeited the appearance so well , that
he grew into great credit , married into a
good family , and by laying out his sudden
stores discreetly , as he saw occasion , and

E 3

joining to all an universal affability, he was admitted to a share of the government of the town, and rose from one post to another, till at length he was closen chief magistrate. In this office he maintained a fair character and continued to fill it with no small applause, both as governor and a judge; till one day as he sat on the bench with some of his brethren, a criminal was brought before him, who was accused of murdering his master. The evidence came out full, the jury brought in their verdict that the prisoner was guilty, and the whole assembly waited the sentence of the president of the court (which he happened to be that day) with great suspense. Mean while he appeared to be in unusual disorder and agitation of mind, his colour changed often; at length he arose from his seat, and coming down from the bench, placed himself just by the unfortunate man at the bar, to the no small astonishment of all present. « You see before you, » said he, addressing himself to those who had sat on the bench with him, « a striking instance of the just awards of heaven, which this day, after thirty years conceal-ment, presents to you a greater criminal than the man just now found guilty ». Then he made an ample confession of his guilt, and of all its aggravations. « Nor can I feel, » continued he, « any relief from the agonies of an awakened conscience, but by requiring that justice be forthwith done against me in the most public and solemn manner. »

We may easily suppose the amazement of all the assembly, and especially of his fellow judges. However, they proceeded, upon his confession, to pass sentence upon him, and he died with all the symptoms of a penitent mind.

M. D. Fordyce in his Dialogues on Education, vol. ii. p. 401. says the above is a true story, and happened in a neighbouring state not many years ago.

CONSTANCY.
SENTIMENTS.

CONSTANCY of mind gives a man reputation, and makes him happy in despite of all misfortunes.

There is not on earth a spectacle more worthy the regard of the Creator, intent on his works , than a brave man superior to his sufferings.

What can be more honourable than to have courage enough to execute the commands of reason and conscience ; to maintain the dignity of our nature , and the station assigned us ; to be proof against poverty , pain , and death itself ? I mean, so far as not to do any thing that is scandalous or sinful to avoid them ; and to stand adversity , under all shapes , with decency and constancy. To do this is to be great above title and fortune. This argues the soul of an heavenly extraction , and is worthy the offspring of the Deity.

Endure and conquer ; Jove will soon dispose
To future good our past and present woes :
An hour will come with pleasure to relate
Your sorrows past , or benefits of fate.—

EXAMPLE.

After the Carthaginians had defeated the Roman army , and taken Regulus , that illustrious commander , prisoner , they met with such a series of misfortunes as induced them to think of putting an end to so destructive a war by a speedy peace. With this view they began to soften the rigour of Regulus's confinement; and endeavoured to engage him to go to Rome with their ambassadors, and to use his interest to bring about a peace upon moderate terms , or at least an exchange of prisoners. Regulus obeyed his masters , and embarked for Rome , after having bound himself , by a solemn oath , to return to his chains , if the negociation did no succeed. The Carthaginian ship arrived safe in Italy : but when Regulus came to the gates of the city , he refused to enter them ; my misfortunes , said he , have made me a slave to the Carthaginians , I am no longer a Roman citizen. The senate always gives audience to foreigners without the gates. His wife Mareia went out to meet him , and presented to him his two children : but he , only casting a wild look on them , fixed his eyes on the ground , as if he thought himself unworthy of the embraces of his wife , and the caresses of his children. When the senators assembled in the suburbs , he was introduced to them with the Carthaginian ambassadors ; and together with them made the two proposals wherewith he was charged. « Conscript fathers , » said he , « being now a slave to the Carthaginians, I am come to treat with you concerning a peace , and an exchange of prisoners. » Having uttered these words, he began to withdraw , and follow the ambassadors , who were not allowed to be present at the deliberations and disputes of the conscript fathers. In vain the senate pressed him to stay. He gave his opinion as an old senator and consul, and refused to continue in the assembly till his African masters ordered him : and then the illustrious slave took his place among the fathers ; but continued silent , with his eyes fixed on the ground , while the more ancient senators spoke. When it came to his turn to deliver his opinion , he addressed himself to the conscript fathers in the following words : « Though I am a slave at Carthage , yet I am free at Rome ; and will therefore declare my sentiments with freedom. Romans, it is not for your interest either to grant the Carthaginians a peace , or to make an exchange of prisoners with them. Carthage is extremely exhausted ; and the only reason why she sues for peace is , because she is not in a condition to continue the war. You have been vanquished but once , and that by my fault ; a fault which Metellus has repaired by a signal victory. But the Cartha-

ginians have been so often overcome, that
they have not the courage to look Rome in
the face. Your allies continue peaceable,
and serve you with zeal. But your enemies
troops consist only of mercenaries, who
have no other tie than that of interest, and
will soon be disobliged by the republic they
serv Carthage being already quite destitute
of money to pay them. No, Romans, a peace
with Carthage does not, by any means,
suit your interest, considering the condition
to which the Carthaginians are reduced : I
therefore advise you to pursue the war with
greater vigour than ever. As for the exchange of prisoners, you have among the
Carthaginian captives several officers of distinction, who are young, and may one day
command the enemies armies : but, as for
me, I am advanced in years, and my misfortunes have made me useless. Besides,
what can you expect from soldiers who have
been vanquished and made slaves ? Such
men, like timorous deer that have escaped
out of the hunter's toils, will ever be upon the
alarm, and ready to fly. » The senate, greatly
affected with his disinterestedness, magnanimity, and contempt of life, would willingly have preserved him, and continued

the war in Africa. Some were of opinion, that
in Rome he was not obliged to keep an oath
which had been extorted from him in an
enemy's country. The Pontifex Maximus
himself, being consulted in the case, declared, that Regulus might continue at Rome,
without being guilty of perjury. But the
noble captive, highly offended at this decision, as if his honour and courage were called in question, declared to the senate, who
trembled to hear him speak, that he well knew
what torments were reserved for him at Carthage ; but that he had so much of the true
spirit of a Roman, as to dread less the tortures of a cruel rack than the shame of a dishonourable action, which would follow him
to the grave. » « It is my duty, » said he, « to
return to Carthage ; let the gods take care
of the rest. » This intrepidity made the senate still more desirous of saving such an
hero. All means were made use of to make
him stay, both by the people and the senate.
He would not even see his wife, nor suffer
his children to take their leave of him.
Amidst the lamentations and tears of the
whole city, he embarked with the Carthaginian ambassadors, to return to the place of
his slavery ; with as serene and cheerful a
countenance

countenance as if he had been going to a country-seat for his diversion. The Carthaginians were so enraged against him, that they invented new torments to satisfy their revenge. First they cut off his eye-lids; keeping him for a while in a dark dungeon, and then bringing him out, and exposing him to the sun ███ noon-day. After this, they shut him up in a kind of a chest, stuck with nails, having their points inwards, so that he could neither sit nor lean, without great torment; and there they suffered him to die with hunger, anguish, and want of sleep.

VAL. MAX. lib. i. c. i. and lib. ix. c. 2. LIV. EPIT. c. xviii. CIC. DE OFFIC. lib. iii. A. GELLIUS, lib. iv.

CONTINENCE.

SENTIMENTS.

CONTINENCE consists not in an insensibility or freedom from passions, but in the well-ordering them.

One man may be much more cheaply virtuous than another, according to the different strength of their passions.

F

The pleasure of subduing an inordinate desire, or denying an impetuous appetite, is not only nobler, but greater by far than any that is to be found in the most transporting moments of gratification.

EXAMPLE.

Scipio the younger, when only twenty-four years of age, was appointed by the Roman republic to the command of the army against the Spaniards. His wisdom and valour would have done honour to the most experienced general. Determined to strike an important blow, he forms a design of besieging Carthagena, then the capital of the Carthaginian empire in Spain. His measures were so judiciously concerted, and with so much courage and intrepidity pursued, both by sea and land, that notwithstanding a bold and vigorous defence, the capital was taken by storm. The plunder was immense. Ten thousand freemen were made prisoners: and above three hundred more, of both sexes, were received as hostages. One of the latter, a very ancient lady, the wife of Mandonius, brother of Indibiles, king of the Hergetes, watching her opportunity, came out of the crowd , and throwing herself at the conqueror's feet , conjured him , with tears in her eyes , to recommend to those who had the ladies in their keeping to have regard to their sex and birth. Scipio , who did not understand her meaning at first , assured her that he had given orders that they should not want for any thing. But the lady replied , « Those conveniences are not what affect us. In the condition to which fortune has reduced us , with what ought we not to be contented ? I have many other apprehensions when I consider , on one side , the licentiousness of war ; and, on the other, the youth and beauty of the princesses, which you see here before us ; for as to me , my age protects me from all fear in this respect. » She had with her the daughters of Indibiles, and several other ladies of high rank , all in the flower of youth , who considered her as their mother. Scipio , then comprehending what the subject of her fear was , « My own glory , » says he , « and that of the Roman people , are concerned in not suffering that virtue, which ought always to be respected, wherever we find it , should be exposed in my camp to a treatment unworthy of it. But you give me a new motive for being more

strict in my care of it , in the virtuous solicitude you shew in thinking only of the preservation of your honour , in the midst of
so many other objects of fear. » After this
conversation, he committed the care of the ladies to some officers of experienced prudence,
strictly commanding , that they should treat
them with all the respect they could pay to the
mothers , wives and daughters of their allies
and particular friends. It was not long before
Scipio's integrity and virtue were put to the
trial. Being retired in his camp , some of his
officers brought him a young virgin of such
exquisite beauty , that she drew upon her
the eyes and admiration of every body. The
young conqueror started from his seat with
confusion and surprize ; and , like one thun-
derstruck , seemed to be robbed of that presence of mind and self-possession so necessary in a general , and for which Scipio was
remarkably famous. In a few moments , having rallied his straggling spirits , he enquired of the beautiful captive , in the most civil
and polite manner , concerning her country,
birth and connections ; and finding that she
was betrothed to a Celtiberian prince, named
Allucius , he ordered both him and the captive's parents to be sent for. The Spanish

prince no sooner appeared in his presence,
than, even before he spoke to the father and
mother, he took him aside; and, to remove
the anxiety he might be in on account of the
young lady, he addressed him in these words:
« You and I are young, which admits of
my speaking to you with more liberty. Those
who brought me your future spouse, assur—
ed me, at the same time, that you loved
her with extreme tenderness: and her
beauty left me no room to doubt it. Upon
which reflecting, that if, like you, I had
thought on making an engagement, and were
not wholly engrossed with the affairs of my
country, I should desire that so honourable
and legitimate a passion should find favour.
I think myself happy in the present conjuncture to do you this service. Though the
fortune of war has made me your master, I
desire to be your friend. Here is your wife :
take her, and may the gods bless you with
her. One thing, however, I would have
you be fully assured of, that she has been
amongst us as she would have been in the
house of her father and mother. Far be it
from Scipio to purchase a loose and momen—
tary pleasure at the expence of virtue, honour, and the happiness of an honest man.

F 3

No : I have kept her for you , in order to make you a present worthy of you and of me. The only gratitude I require of you for this inestimable gift is , that you would be a friend to the Roman people. » Allucius's heart was too full to make him any answer : but throwing himself at the general's feet he wept aloud. The captive lady fell in the same posture ; and remained so , till the father burst out into the following words : « Oh ! divine Scipio ! the gods have given you more than human virtue ! Oh ! glorious leader ! Oh ! wondrous youth ! does not that obliged virgin give you , while she prays to the gods for your prosperity , raptures above all the transports you could have reaped from the possession of her injured person ! »

The relations of the young lady had brought with them a very considerable sum for her ransom : but when they saw that she was restored to them in so generous and godlike a manner , they intreated the conqueror with great earnestness , to accept that sum as a present ; and declared , by his complying , that new favour would complete their joy and gratitude. Scipio , not being able to resist such warm and earnest solicitations , told them , that he accepted

the gift ; and ordered it to be laid at his feet :
then addressing himself to Allucius , «I add,»
says he , « to the portion which you are to receive from your father--in--law this sum ;
which I desire you to accept as a marriage
present. »

If we consider that Scipio was at this time
in the prime of life unmarried , and under no
restraint , we cannot but acknowledge , that
the conquest he made on himself was far
more glorious than that of the Carthaginian
empire. Nor was his virtue unrewarded. The
young prince , charmed whith the liberality
and politeness of Scipio , went into his country to publish the praises of so generous a
victor. He cried out , in the transports of his
gratitude , « That there was come into Spain
a young hero like the gods , who conquered
all things less by the force of his arms , than
the charms of his virtue , and the greatness
of his beneficence. » Upon this all Celtiberia
submitted to the Romans ; and Allucius returned in a shout to Scipio , at the head of
fourteen hundred chosen horse, to facilitate
his future conquests. To render the marks of
his gratitude still more durable , Allucius
caused the action we have just related to be
engraven on a silver shield , which he pre-

sented to Scipio ; a present infinitely more estimable and glorious than all his tresaures and triumphs. This buckler , which Scipio carried whith him when he returned to Rome , was lost , in passing the Rhone , with part of the baggage. It continued in that river , till the year 1665 , when some fishermen found it. It is now in the king of F⸺ce's cabinet.

LIV. lib. xxvi. c. 5o. VAL. MAX. lib. iv. c. 3. ROLLIN's ROM. HIST. vol. 5. p. 382. TATLER , Numb. 58.

C O U R A G E.

S E N T I M E N T S.

A MAN cannot answer for his courage who has never been in danger.

Perfect courage consists in doing without witnesses , all we should be capable of doing before the whole world.

Courage is always just and humane.

Courage without conduct is like fancy without judgment ; all sail and no ballast.

To die or conquer proves a hero's heart.

Presence of mind , and courage in distress ,
Are more than armies to procure success.
True courage dwells not in a troubled flood ,
Of mounting spirits and fermenting blood ,
Lodg'd in the soul , with virtue over-rul'd ,
Inflam'd by reason, and by reason cool'd :
In hours of peace content to be unknown. —

EXAMPLES.

Porsenna , the most potent king then in
Italy , having undertaken to restore the Tarquins to the throne of Rome, from which
they had been banished for their cruelty and
oppression , sent proposals to the senate for
that purpose : but finding they were rejected
with scorn , he advanced towards Rome in a
confident persuasion that he should easily
reduce it. When he came to the bridge ,
and saw the Romans drawn up in order of
battle before the river , he was surprised at
their resolution , and not doubting but he
should overpower them with numbers ,
prepared to fight. The two armies being engaged , fought with great bravery , and long
contended for victory. After a great slaughter
on both sides , the Romans began to give
way , and were quickly put to flight. All
fled into the city over the bridge , which at
the same time would have afforded a passage

to the enemy , if Rome had not found , in the heroic courage of one of her citizens , a bulwark as strong as the highest walls. Pu- blius Horatius was the man , surnamed Co- cles , because he had but one eye , having lost the other in a battle. He used every method to stop the flying army ; but per- ceiving that neither intreaties nor exhorta- tions could overcome their fear , he resolved, however badly supported he might be , to defend the entrance of the bridge till it was demolished behind. On the success of this depended the preservation of the city. Only two Romans followed his example , and partook of his danger : nay , when he saw but a few planks of the bridge remaining, he obliged them to retire , and to save them- selves. Standing alone against a whole army, but preserving his intrepidity , he even dared to insult his numerous enemies ; and cast terrible looks upon the principal Hetru- rians , one while challenged them to a single combat , and then bitterly reproached them all. « Vile slaves that you are, » said he, « not satified with being unmindful of your own , ye are come to deprive others of their liberty who have had the courage to assume it. » Covered with his buckler , he sustained a shower of darts; and at last, when they were all preparing to rush upon him, the bridge was entirely demolished, and Cocles, throwing himself with his arms into the Tyber, safely swam over having performed an action, says Livy, that will command the admiration more than the faith of posterity. He was received as in triumph by the Romans. The people erected him a brazen statue in armour in the most conspicuous part of the Forum. As much land was given him as he could surround with a plough in a day. All the inhabitants, both men and women contributed to his reward; and in the midst of a dreadful scarcity, almost every person in the city, depriving themselves of a part of their subsistence, made him a present of provisions.

LIV. lib. ii. c. 11.

John III. duke of Britany dying without issue, left his dominions to his niece Jane, married to Charles de Blois nephew to the king of France; but John de Mounfort, brother to the late duke, though by a second marriage, claimed the dutchy, and was received as successor by the people of Nantes. The greatest part of the nobility swore fealty to Charles de Blois, thinking him best supported. This dispute occasioned a civil war: in the course of which John was taken prisoner, and sent to Paris. This misfortune would have entirely ruined his party, had not his interest been supported by the extraordinary abilities of his wife, Jane of Flanders, a lady who seems to have possessed in her own person all the excellent qualities of both sexes. Bold, daring, and intrepid, she fought like a warrior in the field: shrewd, sensible, and sagacious, she spoke like a politician in the council, and endowed with the most amiable manners, and winning address, she was able to move the minds of her subjects by the force of her eloquence, and mould them exactly according to her pleasure. She happened to be at Rennes when she received the news of her husband's captivity; but that disaster, instead of depressing her spirits, served only to rouze her native courage and fortitude. She forthwith assembled the citizens, and holding in her arms her infant son, recommended him to their care and protection in the most pathetic terms, as the male heir of their ancient dukes, who had always governed them with lenity and indulgence,

and

and to whom they had ever professed the most zealous attachment. She declared herself willing to run all hazards with them in so just a cause; pointed out the resources that still remained in the alliance of England; earnestly beseeching them to make one vigorous effort against an usurp▓▓▓ who being forced upon them by the intrigues of France, would, as a mark of his gratitude, sacrifice the liberties of Brittany to his protector. The people, moved by the affecting appearance, and animated by the noble conduct of the princess, vowed to live and die with her in defending the rights of her family, and their example was followed by almost all the Bretons. The countess went from place to place, encouraging the garrisons of the several fortresses, and providing them with every thing necessary for their subsistence: after which she shut herself up with her son in Hennebon, where she resolved to wait for the succours which the king of England (Edward III.) had promised to send to her assistance. Charles de Blois accompanied by the dukes of Burgundy and Bourbon, and many other noblemen, took the field with a numerous army, and having reduced Rennes, laid siege to Hen-

nebon , which was defended by the countess in person. This heroine repulsed the
assailants in all their attacks with the most
undaunted courage , and observing one day
that their whole army had left the camp to
join in a general storm, she rushed forth at a
postern-gate , with three hundred horse , set
fire to their tents and baggage , killed their
sutlers and servants , and raised such a terror and consternation through all their quar-
ters , that the enemy gave over their assault
and getting betwixt her and the walls , endeavoured to cut off her retreat to the city.
Thus intercepted , she put the spurs to her
horse , and , without halting , galloped directly to Brest , which lay at the distance of
two-and-twenty miles from the scene of action. There being supplied with a body of
five hundred horse , she immediately returned , and fighting her way through one part
of the French camp, was received into Hennebon , amidst the acclamations of the people. Soon after this the English succours
appeared , and obliged the enemy to raise
the siege.

RAPIN. RIDER'S HIST. ENG. vol. xlv.
p. 6—17.

DISINTERESTEDNESS.

SENTIMENTS.

He who in good time firmly renounces a great name, great authority, or a great fortune, delivers himself at once from a host of troubles, from many restless nights, and what is still better, often from many crimes.

Many unjust grow rich, and pious poor;
We would not change our virtue for their store:
For constant virtue is a solid base,
Riches from man to man uncertain pass.

Let no price or promises bribe thee to take part with the enemies of thy prince; whoever wins thou art lost. If thy prince prosper, thou art proclaimed a rebel, and must expect the consequence; if the enemy prevail, thou art reckoned but a meritorious traitor: though he may like and love thy treason, yet he will hate and despise thee.

Nothing is a greater argument of a brave soul, and impregnable virtue, than for a man to be so much master of himself, that

G 2

he can either take or leave those conveniences of life , with respect to which most are
either uneasy without them, or intemperate
with them.

E X A M P L E S.

The deputies of Philip , king of Macedon ,
offering great sums of money in that prince's
name to Phocion , the Athenian , and in-
treating him to accept them , if not for himself , at least for his children , who were in
such circumstances that it would be impossible for them to support the glory of his
name : « If they resemble me , » said Phocion , « the little spot of ground , with the
produce of which I have hitherto lived , and
which has raised me to the glory you mention , will be sufficient to maintain them :
if it will not , I do not intend to have them
wealthy merely to foment and heighten their
luxury. » Alexander the great , son of Philip , having sent him an hundred talents ,
Phocion asked those who brought them ,
upon what design Alexander had sent him
so great a sum , and did not remit any to
the rest of the Athenians ? « It is , », replied
they , « because Alexander looks upon you

as the most just and virtuous man. » Says Phocion , « Let him suffer me still to enjoy that character, and be really what I am taken for. »

COR. NEPOS. IN PHOC.

STRABO , king of the Sidonians , having declared in favour of Darius , the Persian monarch , Alexander the Great expelled him the kingdom , and permitted Hephæstion , his beloved friend , to give the crown to whomsoever of the Sidonians he should judge worthy of so exalted a station. This favourite was quartered at the house of two brothers , who were young and of the most considerable family in the city : to these he offered the crown , but they declined to accept it , telling him , that according to the laws of their country, no person could ascend the throne, unless he were of the blood royal. Hephæstion admiring this greatness of soul , which could contemn what others strive to obtain by fire and sword , « Continue, » says he to them, « in this way of thinking ; you who before were sensible that it was much more glorious to refuse a diadem than to accept it. However , name me some person of the royal family, who may remem-

G 3

ber , when he is king , that it was you who set the crown on his head. » The brothers observing , that several through excessive ambition aspired to this high station , and to obtain it paid a servile court to Alexander's favourites , declared that they did not know any person more worthy of the diadem than one Abdolonymus , descended , though at a great distance , from the royal line ; but who at the same time was so poor , that he was obliged to get his bread by day-labour in a garden without the city. His honesty and integrity had reduced him , as well as many more , to this extreme poverty. Immediately the two brothers went in search of Abdolonymus with the royal garments , and found him weeding his garden; they then saluted him king , and one of them addressed him thus : You must now change your tatters for the dress I have brought you. Put off the mean and contemptible habit in which you have grown old. Assume the sentiments of a prince ; but when you are seated on the throne , continue to preserve the virtue which made you worthy of it ; and when you shall have ascended it , and by that means become the supreme dispenser of life and death over all your citizens , be sure to forget the condition in which, or rather for which you was elected. » Abdolonymus looked upon the whole as a dream, and, unable to guess the meaning of it, asked, if they were not ashamed to ridicule him in that manner? But as he made a greater resistance than suited their inclinations, they themselves washed him, and threw over his shoulders a purple robe, richly embroidered with gold; then, after repeated oaths of their being in earnest, they conducted him to the palace. The news of this was immediately spread over the whole city. Most of the inhabitants were overjoyed at it; but some murmured, especially the rich, who despising Abdolonymus's former abject state, could not forbear shewing their resentment upon that account in the king's court. Alexander commanded the new elected prince to be sent for; and after surveying him attentively a long while, spoke thus; Thy air and mein do not contradict what is related of thy extraction; but I should be glad to know with what frame of mind thou didst bear thy poverty. » — « Would to the gods, » replied he, « that I may bear this crown with equal patience. These hands have procured me all I desired; and whilst I possessed nothing, I

wanted nothing. This answer gave Alexander an high idea of Abdolonymus's virtue :
so that he presented him not only with all
the rich furniture which had belonged to
Strabo and part of the Persian plunder , but
likewise annexed one of the neighbouring
provinces to his dominions.

     Q. Curt. lib. iv. c. i. and lib. viii. c. 14.

  When Bresse was taken by storm from the
Venetians , the chevalier Bayard saved a
house from plunder , whither he had retired
to have a dangerous wound drest which he
received in the siege , and secured the mistress of the family and her two daughters
who were hid in it. At his departure the
lady , as a mark of her gratitude , offered
him a casket containing two thousand five
hundred ducats , which he obstinately refused. But observing , that his refusal was
displeasing to her , and not caring to leave
her dissatisfied, he consented to accept of her
present , and calling to him the two young
ladies to take his leave of them, he presented
each of them with a thousand ducats , to be
added to their portion, and left the remaining
five hundred to be distributed among the
inhabitants that had been plundered.

       Vie du Chev. Bayard.

But that we may have a better notion of the nobleness and greatness of a disinterested mind , let us consider , not in generals and princes , whose glory and power may seem perhaps to heighten the lustre of this virtue , but in persons of a lower rank , who have nothing about them but the virtue itself to raise our admiration. A poor man , who was door-keeper to a boarding house in Milan, found a purse with two hundred crowns in it. The man who had lost it , informed by a public advertisement, came to the house, and giving good proof that the purse belonged to him , the door-keeper restored it to him. The owner full of joy and gratitude , offered his benefactor twenty crowns, which the other absolutely refused. He then came down to ten, and afterwards to five, but finding him still inexorable , he throws his purse upon the ground , and in an angry tone , « I have lost nothing , » says he , « nothing at all, if you thus refuse to accept of any thing.» The door-keeper then accepted of five crowns, which he immediately distributed among the poor.

ROLLIN'S BELLES LETT.

D R U N K E N N E S S.

S E N T I M E N T S.

IT is very common that events arise from a debauch which are fatal, and always such as are disagreeable. With all a man's reason and good sense about him, his tongue is apt to utter things out of mere gaiety of heart, which may displease his best friends. Who then would trust himself to the power of wine, if there was no other objection against it than this, that it raises the imagination, and depresses the judgment.

However this tribe of people may think of themselves, a drunken man is a greater monster than any that is to be found amongst all the creatures which God has made, as indeed there is no character which appears more despicable and depraved, in the eyes of all reasonable persons, than that of a drunkard.

E X A M P L E S.

Cyrus according to the manners of the Persians, was from his infancy accustomed to sobriety and temperance ; of which he was himself a most illustrious example through the whole course of his life. When Cyrus was twelve years old , his mother Mandana took him with her into Media , to his grandfather Astyages , who from the many things he had heard said in favour of th██████ung prince , had a great desire to see him. In this court young Cyrus found very different manners from those of his own country : pride , luxury , and magnificence , reigned here universally ; all which did not affect Cyrus , who without criticising or condemning what he saw , was contented to live as he had been brought up , and adhered to the principles he had imbibed from his infancy. He charmed his grandfather by his sprightliness and wit ; and gained every body's favour by his noble and engaging behaviour. Astyages , to make his grandson unwilling to return home , made a sumptuous entertainment , in which there was a vast plenty and profusion of every thing that was nice and delicate. All this exquisite cheer and magnificent preparation Cyrus looked upon with great indifference. «The Persians,» says he to the king , « instead of going such a round-about-way to appease their hunger, have a much shorter to the same end ; a little bread and a few cresses with them answer the purpose. » Astyages desiring Cyrus to dispose of all the meats as he thought fit, the latter immediately distributed them to the king's officers in waiting ; to one, because he taught him to ride ; to another, because he waited well upon his grandfather ; and to a third, because he took great care of his mother. Sacras the king's cup–bearer, was the only person to whom he gave nothing. This officer, besides the post of cup-bearer, had that likewise of introducing those who were to have an audience of the king ; and as he did not grant that favour to Cyrus as often as he desired it, he had the misfortune to displease the prince, who took this occasion to shew his resentment. Astyages, testifying some concern at the neglect of this officer, for whom he had a particular regard ; and who deserved it, as he said, on account of the wonderful dexterity with which he served him : « Is that all, Sir ? » replied Cyrus, « if that be sufficient to merit your favour, you shall see I will quickly obtain it ; for I will take upon me to serve you better than he. » Immediately Cyrus is equipped as a cup - bearer ; and advancing gravely

gravely, with a serious countenance, a napkin upon his shoulder, and holding the cup nicely with three of his fingers, he presented it to the king, with a dexterity and grace that charmed both Astyages and his mother Mandana. When he had done, he flung himself upon his grandfather's neck, and kissing him, cried out with great joy, » O Sacras, poor Sacras, thou art undone; I shall have thy place. » Astyages embraced him with great fondness, and said, « I am mighty well pleased, my son; nobody can serve with a better grace : but you have forgot one essential ceremony, which is that of tasting. » And indeed the cup-bearer was used to pour some of the liquor into his left-hand, and to taste it, before he presented it to the king. « No, » replied Cyrus; « it was not through forgetfulness that I omitted that ceremony. » « Why then, » says Astyages; « for what reason did you omit it? » « Because I apprehended there was poison in the liquor. » « Poison, child! how could you think so? » « Yes, poison, papa : for not long ago, at an entertainment you gave to the lords of your court, I perceived all their heads were turned : they sung, made a noise, and talked they did not know what; you yourself seemed

H

to have forgotten that you were a king , and
they that they were subjects , and when you
would have danced you could not stand upon
your legs. » « Why, » says Astyages : « have
you never seen the same thing happen to
your father ? » « No , never , » says Cyrus.
« What then ; how is it with him when he
drinks ? » « Why , when he has drank , his
thirst is quenched ; and that is all. »

XENOPH. CYR. lib. i.

Clitus was one of Alexander's best friends,
an old officer , who had fought under his father Philip , and signalized himself on many
occasions. At the battle of the Granicus , as
Alexander was fighting bare-headed , and
Rosaces had his arm raised in order to strike
him behind , he covered the king with his
shield : and cut off the barbarian's hand.
Hellenice his sister , had nursed Alexander;
and he loved her with as much tenderness
as if she had been his own mother. As the
king , from these several considerations , had
a very great respect for Clitus , he intrusted
him with the government of one of the most
important provinces of his empire : and ordered him to set out the next day. In the
evening , Clitus was invited to an enter-

tainment, in which the king, after drinking to excess, began to celebrate his own exploits; and was so excessively lavish of self — commendation, that he even shocked those very persons who knew what he spoke was in general true. Clitus, who by this time, as well as the rest of the company, w████ually intoxicated, began to relate the actions of Philip, and his wars in Greece, preferring them to whatever was done by Alexander. Though the king was prodigiously vexed, he nevertheless stifled his resentment; and it is probable that he would have quite suppressed his passion, had Clitus stopped thère; but the latter growing more and more talkative, as if determined to exasperate and insult the king, he was commanded to leave the table. « He is in the right (says Clitus, as he rose up) not to bear free — born men at his table, who can only tell him truth. He will do well to pass his life among barbarians and slaves, who will pay adoration to his Persian girdle, and his white robe. The king, no longer able to suppress his rage, snatched a javelin from one of the guards, and would have killed Clitus on the spot, had not the courtiers withheld his arm, and Clitus been forced,

H 2

with great difficulty , out of the hall. However , he returned into it that moment by another door , singing , with an air of insolence , verses reflecting highly on the prince , who seeing the general near him , struck him with his javelin dead at his feet, crying out , at the same time , « Go now to Philip, to Parmenio , and to Attalus. »

As soon as the king was capable of reflecting seriously on what he had done , his crime displayed itself to him in the blackest and most dreadful light : for though Clitus had committed a great and inexcusable fault, yet it must be confessed , that the circumstances of the banquet extenuate in some degree , or throw , in some measure , a veil over Clitus's conduct. When a king makes a subject his companion in a debauch , he seems , on such an occasion , to forget his dignity , and to permit his subjects to forget it also : he gives a sanction , as it were, to the liberties, familiarities , and sudden flights which wine commonly inspires. A fault committed under these circumstances , is always a fault ; but then it ought never to be expiated with the blood of the offender. This Alexander had generosity enough to acknowledge; and at the same time , perceived that he had done the vile office of an executioner in punishing , by an horrid murder , the uttering some indis—creet words which ought to be imputed to the fumes of wine. Upon this , he threw himself upon his friend's body , forced out the javelin , and would have dispatched himself with it , had he not been prevented by his g████. He passed that night and the next day in tears , stretched on the ground , and venting only groans and deep sighs.

Q. CURT. PLUT. IN ALEX. JUST. lib. xii. c. 6. 7.

E Q U I T Y.

S E N T I M E N T S.

Equity is the band of human society ; a kind of tacit agreement and impression of nature , without which there is not any thing we do that can deserve commendation.

Equity judges with lenity , laws with ex—tremity. In all moral cases , the reason of the law is in the law.

Equity consists in an exact and scrupulous regard to the rights of others , with a delibe—rate purpose to preserve them on all occa—

H 3

sions sacred and inviolate. — And from this fair and equitable temper, performing every necessary act of justice that relates to their persons or properties; being just to their infirmities, making all the allowance in their favour which their circumstances require, and a good–natured and equitable construction of particular cases will admit of; being true to our friendships, to our promises and contracts: just in our traffic, just in our demands, and just by observing a due moderation and proportion even in our resentments.

E X A M P L E S.

M. Popilius Lœnas, the Roman consul, being sent against the Stelliates, a people in Liguria, bordering on the river Tanarus, killed and took so many of them prisoners, that finding the forces of their nation reduced to ten thousand men, they submitted to the consul without settling any terms. Upon which Popilius took away their arms, dismantled their cities, reduced them all to slavery, and sold them and their goods to the best bidder. But such was the equity of the Roman senate, that they resented this severe and cruel proceeding, and passed a decree, commanding Popilius to restore the money he had received for the sale of the Stelliates, to set them at liberty, return to them their effects, and even to purchase new arms for them : and concluded their decree with words which posterity ought never to forget, « Victory is glorious, when it is confined to the subduing of an untractable enemy ; but it becomes shameful when it is made use of to oppress the unfortunate. »

Liv. lib. xliii. c. 8.

Trajan, the Roman emperor, would never suffer any one to be condemned upon suspicions, however strong and well-grounded ; saying, it was better a thousand criminals should escape unpunished than one innocent person be condemned. When he appointed Subarranus captain of his guards, to present him, according to custom, with a drawn sword, the badge of his office, he used these memorable words : *Pro me ; si merear, in me*: « Employ this sword for me ; but turn it, if I deserve it, against me. »

Dio. p. 778.

He allowed none of his freedmen any share in the administration, telling them, that *he* , and not *they* , was invested with the sovereign power ; and therefore warning them not to assume any authority inconsistent with their rank. Some persons having a suit with one of them , Eurythmus , and seeming to fear an imperial freedman, Trajan assured them that the cause should be heard, discussed and decided , according to the strictest laws of justice ; adding , « For neither is he Polycletus nor I Nero. » *Polycletus* was that cruel prince's freedman , infamous for his rapine and injustice.

The same excellent prince , having assumed the fasces, in the presence of the people , bound himself by a solemn oath to observe the laws , declaring , « That what was forbidden to private citizens was equally forbidden to princes , who as they are not above the laws , are no less bound than the meanest of the populace to conform to them. Hence to the public vows , which were in the beginning of each year offered for the health and prosperity of the emperor , he added these conditions : « *if he observes the laws ; if he governs the republic as he ought ; if he procures the happiness of the people.*

PLIN. PANEG. p. 134.

The Persians thought it reasonable to put the good as well as the evil , the merits of the offender as well as the demerits into the scales of justice : nor was it just in their opinion , that one single crime should obliterate all the good actions a man had done during his life ; because it might rather be considered as an effect of human frailty , than of a confirmed malignity of mind. Upon this principle it was that Darius , having condemned a judge to death for some prevarication in his office , and afterwards , calling to mind the important services he had rendered both the state and the royal family , revoked the sentence , at the very moment of its going to be executed ; and acknowledged , that he had pronounced it with more precipitation than wisdom. But one important and essential rule which they observed in their judgments was , in the first place , never to condemn any person without bringing his accuser to his face , and without giving him time, and all other means necessary for defending himself against the articles laid to his charge ; and in the second place , if the person accused was found innocent , to inflict the very same punishment upon the accuser as the other was to have

suffered, had he been found guilty. Artaxer-
xes gave a fine example of the just rigour
that ought to be exercised on such occasions.
One of the king's favourites, ambitious of
getting a place possessed by one of his best
officers, endeavoured to make the king sus-
pect the fidelity of that officer, and to that
end sent information to court full of calumnies
against him, persuading himself that the
king, from the great credit he had with his
majesty, would believe the thing upon his
bare word, without further examination.
Such is the general character of calumniators.
— They are afraid of evidence and light, and
make it their business to shut out the in-
nocents from all recesses to their prince, and
thereby put it out of their power to vindi-
cate themselves. The officer was imprisoned : but he desired of the king, before he
was condemned, that his cause might be
heard, and his accusers ordered to produce
their evidence against him. The king did so :
and as there was no proof but the letters
which his enemy had written against him,
he was cleared, and his innocence fully justi-
fied, by the three commissioners that sat
upon his trial. All the king's indignation fell
upon the perfidious accuser, who had thus

attempted to abuse the favour and confidence of his royal master. This prince, who was very wise, and knew that one of the true signs of a prudent government was to have the subjects stand more in awe of the law than of informers, would have thought an opposite conduct a direct violation of one of the most common rules of natural equity and humanity. It would have been opening a door to envy, hatred, and revenge; it would have been exposing the honest simplicity of good and faithful subjects to the cruel malice of detestable informers, and arming these with the sword of public authority; in a word, it would have been divesting the throne of the most noble privilege belonging to it, namely, of being a sanctuary for-innocence, against violence and calumny.

HEROD. lib. vii. c. 194.

FLATTERY.

SENTIMENTS.

Nothing misbecomes
The man that would be thought a friend, like flatt'ry;
Flattr'y, the meanest kind of base dissembling,
And only used to catch the grossest fools.

Please not thyself the flattering crowd to hear ;
'Tis fulsome stuff, to please thy itching ear.
Survey thy soul : not what thou dost appear ,
But what art thou —

THE heart has no avenue so open as that of flattery , which , like some enchantment , lays all its guards asleep.

Nothing sinks a great character so much as raising it above credibility.

He that reviles me (it may be) calls me fool ; but he that flatters me , if I take not heed , will make me one.

Satisfaction can no where be placed but in a just sense of our own integrity , without regard to the opinions of others.

The only coin that is most current among mankind is flattery : the only benefit of which is that , by hearing what we are not , we may learn what we ought to be.

E X A M P L E S.

WHEN Ptolemy Euergetes first set out on his expedition into Syria , his queen Berenice , who tenderly loved him , being apprehensive of the dangers to which he might be exposed in the war , made a vow to consecrate her hair , which was her chief ornament , in case he should return safe. The

prince

prince returned not only safe, but crowned with glory and success; whereupon Berenice, to discharge her vow, immediately cut off her hair, and dedicated it to the gods, in the temple which Ptolomy Philadelphus had built in honour of his beloved Arsinol, under the name of the Zephyrian Venus, on the promontory of Zephyrium, in Cyprus. But this consecrated hair being lost soon after, or perhaps contemptuously flung away by the priests, Ptolemy was much offended at this accident, and threatened to punish the priests for their neglect. Hereupon Conon of Samos, a flattering courtier, and great mathematician, to appease the king's wrath, and gain his favour, gave out that the queen's locks had been conveyed up to heaven; and pointed out seven stars, which, till that time, had not belonged to any constellation, declaring, that they were the queen's hair. Several other astronomers, either to make their court, as well as Conon to the king, or out of fear of drawing upon themselves his displeasure, affirmed the same thing; and hence *coma Berenices*, or the hair of Berenice, became one of the constellations, and is so to this day.

HYGINI POETIC. ASTRONOM.

I

Prusias, king of Bithynia, being come to Rome to make the senate and Roman people his compliments of congratulation upon the good success of the war against Perseus, dishonoured the royal dignity by abject flattery. At his reception by the deputies appointed by the senate for that purpose, he appeared with his head shaved, and with the cap, habit, shoes and stockings of a slave made free; and, saluting the deputies, «You see,» said he, «one of your freedmen ready to fulfil whatever you shall choose to command, and to conform entirely to all your customs.» When he entered the senate he stopped at the door, facing the senators, who sat, and prostrating himself, kissed the threshold. Afterwards, addressing himself to the assembly, « I salute you, gods, preservers,» cried he; and went on with a discourse suitable to that prelude. Polybius says that he was ashamed to repeat it, and well he might; for that base deportment, at least dishonoured as much the senate, who suffered, as the prince who acted it.

POLYBIUS, leget. 97.

Antiochus Sidetes, king of Syria, was a prince estimable for many excellent quali—

ties. As a proof of his wisdom, he detested flattery. One day, having lost himself a hunting, and being alone, he rode up to the cottage of a poor family, who received him in the best manner they could, without knowing him. At supper, having himself turned the conversation upon the conduct and character of the king, they said, that he was in every thing else a good prince, but that his too great passion for hunting made him neglect the affairs of his kingdom, and repose too much confidence in his courtiers, whose actions did not always correspond with the goodness of his intentions; Antiochus made no answer at that time. The next day, upon the arrival of his train at the cottage, he was known. He repeated to his attendants what had passed the evening before; and told them by way of reproach. « Since I have taken you into my service, I have not heard a truth concerning myself till yesterday ».

PLUT. IN APOPHTEGM, p. 185.

As Canute the Great, king of England, was walking on the sea-shore at Southampton, accompanied by his courtiers, who offered him the grossest flattery, comparing him to the greatest heroes of antiquity, and assert—

I 2

ing that his power was more than human , he
ordered a chair to be placed on the beach,
while the tide was coming in. Sitting down
with a majestic air , he thus addressed himself to the sea : Thou sea , that art a part
of my dominions , and the land whereon
I sit is mine , no one ever broke my commands with impunity ; I therefore ⬛⬛⬛⬛
thee to come no farther upon my land , and
not to presume to wet either my feet or my
robe , who am thy sovereign. » But the sea ,
rolling on as before , and without any respect, not only wet the skirts of his robe , but
likewise splashed his thighs. On which he
rose up suddenly , and addressing himself
to his attendants , upbraided them with their
ridiculous flattery ; and very judiciously expatiated on the narrow , and limited power
of the greatest monarch on earth.

HUNTINGDON , lib. vi. FLORILEG. IN
A. D. 1035.

F R E E D O M

WITH GREAT MEN DANGEROUS.

SENTIMENTS.

IT is observed in the course of worldly things, that misfortunes are oftener made by men's tongues than by their virtues; and more men's fortunes overthrown thereby than by their vices.

Good counsel is cast away upon the arrogant, the self-conceited, or the stupid, who are either too proud to take it, or too heavy to understand it.

If you be consulted concerning a person either passionate, inconstant, or vicious, give not your advice: it is in vain; for such will do only what shall please themselves.

You are so far from obliging a man by relating to him the ill things which have been said of him, that you are quickly paid for your indiscretion by becoming the first object of his aversion and resentment.

Never assent merely to please, for that betrays a servile mind; nor contradict to

I 3

vex, for that argues an ill temper and ill breeding.

EXAMPLES.

Alexander tha Great, having determined to carry on war with India, the richest country in the world not only in gold, but in pearls and precious stones, with ~~████~~ the inhabitants adorned themselves with more luxury, indeed, than gracefulness, Alexander was informed, that the swords of the soldiers were of gold and ivory; and the king, now the greatest monarch in the world, being determined not to yield to any person whatsoever in any circumstance, caused the swords of his soldiers to be set off with silver plates, put golden bridles to the horses, had the coats of mail heightened with gold and silver; and prepared to march for this enterprise at the head of one hundred and twenty thousand men, all equipped with the magnificence above described.

All things being ready for their setting out, he thought this a proper opportunity to reveal the design he had so long meditated, viz. to have divine honours paid him. To sooth and cherish this ridiculous pretension, there were not wanting flatterers, those common pests of courts, who are more dangerous to princes than the arms of their enemies. With this view he appointed a festival, and made an incredible pompous banquet : to which he invited the greatest lords of his court, both Macedonians and Greeks, and most of the highest quality among the Persians. With these he sat down at table for some time ; after which he withdrew. Upon this Cleon, one of his flatterers, began to speak ; and expatiated very much on the praises of the king, as had before been agreed upon. He made a long detail of the high obligations they had to him ; all which, he observed, they might acknowledge and repay at a very easy expence, merely with two grains of incense, which they should offer him as to a God, without the least scruple, since they believed him such. To this purpose he cited the example of the Persians ; and added, that in case the rest should not care to pay this justice to Alexander's merit, he himself was resolved to shew them the way, and to worship him in case he should return into the hall. But that all of them must do their duty, especially those who professed wisdom, and ought to serve the rest as an example of the veneration due to so great a monarch. It appeared plainly that this speech was directed to Callisthenes. He was related to Aristotle, who had presented him to Alexander, his pupil, that he might attend upon that monarch in the war of Persia. He was considered, upon account of his wisdom and gravity, as the fittest person to give him such wholesome counsels as were most likely to preserve him from those excesses into which his youth and fiery temper might hurry him. This philosopher seeing that every one on this occasion continued in deep silence, and that the eyes of the whole assembly were fixed upon him, addressed himself to Cleon in the following words: « Had the king been present when thou madest thy speech, none among us would have attempted to answer thee; for he himself would have interrupted thee, and not have suffered thee to prompt him to assume the customs of Barbarians, in casting an odium on his person and glory, by so servile an adulation. But since he is absent, I will answer thee in his name. I consider Alexander as worthy of all the honours that can be paid a mortal; but there is a difference between the worship of the gods and that of men. The former includes tem—

ples, altars, prayers and sacrifices; the latter is confined to commendations only, and
awful respect.

We salute the latter, and look upon it
as glorious to pay them submission, obedience, and fidelity; but we adore the former. We institute festivals to their honour,
and sing hymns and spiritual songs to their
glory. We must not therefore confound
things, either by bringing down the gods to
the condition of mortals, or by raising a
mortal to the state of a god. Alexander
would be justly offended should we pay to
another person the homage due to his sacred person only; ought we not to dread the
indignation of the gods as much, should we
bestow upon mortals the honour due to them
alone? I am sensible that our monarch is
vastly superior to the rest; he is the greatest
of kings, and the most glorious of all conquerors; but then he is a man, not a god. —
The Greeks did not worship Hercules till
after his death; and then not till the oracle
had expressly commanded it. The Persians
are cited as an example for our imitation;
but how long is it that the vanquished have
given law to the victor? Can we forget,
that Alexander crossed the Hellespont, not

to subject Greece to Asia , but Asia to Greece ?

The deep silence which all the company observed whilst Callisthenes spoke was an indication , in some measure , of their thoughts. The king who stood behind the tapestry all the time , heard whatever had passed. He therefore ordered Cleon to be told that , without insisting any farther , he would only require the Persians to fall prostrate , according to their usual custom ; a little after which he came in , pretending he had been busied in some affair of importance. Immediately the Persians fell prostrate to adore him. Polysperchon , who stood near him , observing that one of them bowed so low , that his chin touched the ground , bid him in a rallying tone of voice to strike harder. The king offended at this joke , threw Polysperchon into prison. As for Callisthenes , the king determined to get rid of him , and therefore laid to his charge a crime of which he was no way guilty. Accordingly , he was thrown into a dungeon , loaded with irons , and the most grievous torments were inflicted on him , in order to extort a confession of guilt. But he insisted upon his innocence to the last , and expired in the midst of his tortures.

Nothing has reflected a greater dishonour on Alexander's memory than this unjust and cruel death of Callisthenes ; and by this dreadful example he deprived all virtuous men of the opportunity of exhorting him to ▓▓▓ things which were for his true interest. From that instant no one spoke with freedom in the council ; even those who had the greatest love for the public good , and a personal affection for Alexander, thought themselves not obliged to undeceive him. After this , nothing was listened to but flattery , which gained such an ascendancy over that prince , as entirely depraved him , and justly punished him , for having sacrificed to the wild ambition of having adoration paid him , the most virtuous man about his person. « The murder of this philosopher , » says Seneca , « was a crime of so heinous a nature , as entirely obliterates the glory of all his other actions. »

SENEC. NAT. QUEST. lib. vi. c. 23.

Darius having raised a prodigious army , all richly clothed, himself and the whole court glittering with gold and precious stones , set out to meet Alexander the Great, near the city of Issus. There was at that time in the army of Darius one Caridemus, an Athenian, a man of great experience in war, who personnally hated Alexander for having caused him to be banished from Athens. Darius, turning to this Athenian, asked. whether he believed him powerful enough to defeat his enemy? Caridemus, who had been brought up in the bosom of liberty, and forgetting that he was in a country of slavery, where to oppose the inclination of a prince is of the most dangerous consequence, replied as follows : « Possibly, Sir, you may be displeased with my telling you the truth : but in case I do it not now, it will be too late hereafter. This mighty parade of war, this prodigious number of men, which has drained all the East, might indeed be formidable to your neighbours. Gold and purple shine in every part of your army, which is so prodigiously splendid, that those who have not seen it could never form an idea of its magnificence. But the soldiers who compose the enemy's army, terrible to behold, and bristling in every part with arms, do not amuse themselves with such idle show. Their

Their only care is to discipline in a regular
manner their battalions, and to cover themselves close with their bucklers and pikes.
Their phalanx is a body of infantry, which
engages without flinching, and keeps so
close in their ranks, that the soldier and their
arms, form a kind of impenetrable work. In
a word, every single man among them, the
officers as well as soldiers, are so well trained
up, and so attentive to the command of
their leaders, that at the least signal they
make every motion and evolution of the art
of war. But that you may be persuaded these
Macedonians are not invited hither from the
hopes of gaining gold and silver, know that
this excellent discipline has subsisted
hitherto by the sole aid and precept of poverty. Are they hungry, they satisfy their ap-
petites with any kind of food. Are they weary,
they repose themselves on the bare ground,
and in the day-time are always on their feet.
Do you imagine that the Thessalian cavalry,
and that of Arcarania and Ætolia, who are
all armed cap-a-pee, are to be repulsed by
stones hurled from flings, and with sticks
burned at the end? Such troops as are
like themselves will be able to check their
career; and succours must be provided

K

from their country to oppose their bravery and experience. Send therefore thither all the useless gold and silver which I see here, and purchase formidable soldiers. » Darius was naturally of a mild, tractable temper; but good fortune will corrupt the most happy disposition. Few monarchs are resolute and courageous enough to withstand their power, and to esteem a man who loves them so well, as to contradict and displease them, in telling them the genuine truth. Darius, not having strength of mind sufficient for this, gave order for dragging to execution a man who had fled to him for protection, was at that time his guest, and who gave him the best counsel that could have been proposed to him : however as this cruel treatment could not silence Caridemus, he cried aloud with his usual freedom, « My avenger is at hand, the very man in opposition to whom I gave you counsel, and he will punish you for despising it. As for you, Darius, in whom sovereign power has wrought so sudden a change, you will teach posterity, that when once men abandon themselves to the delusions of fortune, she erases from their minds all the seeds of goodness implanted in them by nature. » Darius soon repented his having put to death so valuable a person ; and experienced , but too late , the truth of all he had told him.

Notwithstanding it is foreign to the design of this collection , yet as the appearance made by Darius and his army was so extremely grand and pompous , an exact description of it may not be disagreeable to some of my young readers.

It was a custom long used by the Persians never to set out upon a march till after sunrise, at which time the trumpet was sounded for that purpose from the king's tent. Over this tent was exhibited to the view of the whole army the image of the sun set in crystal. The order they observed in their march was this : first , they carried silver altars , on which they lay fire, called by them sacred and eternal; and these where followed by the magi , singing hymns , after the manner of their country. They were accompanied by three hundred and sixty-five youths , (agreeable to the number of days in a year) clothed in purple robes ; after them came a chariot , consecrated to their god , drawn by white horses , and followed by a courser of a prodigious size , to whom they gave the name of the sun's horse; and the

K 2

equeries were dressed in white, each having a golden rod in his hand. Ten chariots, adorned with sculptures in gold and silver, followed after. Then marched a body of horse, composed of twelve nations, whose manners and customs were various, and all armed in a different manner. Next advanced those whom the Persians called the immortals, amounting to ten thousand, who surpassed the rest of the Barbarians in the sumptuousness of their apparel. They all wore golden collars, were clothed in robes of gold tissue, with surtouts (having sleeves to them) quite covered with precious stones. Thirty paces from them followed those called the king's cousins or relations, to the number of fifteen thousand, in habits very much resembling those of women, and more remarkable for the vain pomp of their dress, than the glitter of their arms. Those called the doryphori came after; they carried the king's cloak, and walked before his chariot, in which he seemed to sit as on a high throne. This chariot was enriched on both sides with images of the gods, in gold and silver; and from the middle of the yoke, which was covered with jewels, rose two statues, a cubit in height; the one representing war, the other peace, having a golden eagle between them with wings extended, as ready to take its flight. But nothing could equal the magnificence of the king. He was clothed in a vest of purple, striped with silver, and over it a long robe glittering all over with gold and precious stones, that represented two falcons rushing from the clouds and pecking at one another. Around his waist he wore a golden girdle, after the manner of women, whence his scymitar hung, the scabbard of which flamed all over with gems. On his head he wore a tiara or mitre, round which was a fillet of blue, mixed with white. On each side of him walked two hundred of his nearest relations, followed by ten thousand slaves and pikemen, whose pikes were adorned with silver, and tipped with gold; and lastly thirty thousand infantry, who composed the rear guard : these were followed by the king's horses (four hundred in number) all which were led. About one hundred, or an hundred and twenty paces from them, came Sysigambis, Darius's mother; seated on a chariot, and his consort on another, with the several female attendants of both queens riding on horseback. Afterwards came fifteen large chariots; in which were the

K 3

king's children, and those who had the care
of their education, with a band of eunuchs,
who are to this day in great esteem with
those nations. Then marched the concubines to the number of three hundred and sixty,
in the equipage of queens, followed by six
hundred mules, and three hundred camels,
which carried the king's treasure, and were
guarded by a great body of archers. After
these came the wives of the crown-offi-
cers, and of the greatest lords of the court;
then the sutlers and servants of the army,
seated also in chariots. In the rear were a
body of light-armed troops, with their com-
manders, who closed the whole.

Would not any one believe that this was
the description of a tournament rather than
the march of an army? Can it be imagined
that princes possessed of the least reason
would have been so stupid as to incorporate
with their forces so cumbersome a train of
women, princesses, concubines, and domestics of both sexes? But Darius at the
head of six hundred thousand men, and surrounded with this mighty pomp, prepared
for himself only, fancied he was great, and
rose in the idea he had formed of himself;
yet should we reduce him to his just propor-

tion, and his personal worth, how little would he appear!

Q. CURT. ROLL. ANT. HIST. lib. vii.
p. 145.

FRIENDSHIP.

SENTIMENTS.

WITHOUT friendship life has no charm. The only things which can render friendship sure and lasting are, virtue, purity of manners, an elevated soul, and a perfect integrity of heart.

The first rule in the choice of a friend, is not to love him before you know him : almost at first sight we may know if a man be of quick or slow parts, if he be gay or serious, clownish or polite, talkative or reserved, witty or stupid ; we see almost all this in his eyes, in his attitude, in his gestures, and in his discourse ; but we cannot so easily discover whether he has virtue and probity. It requires more time to be certain with regard to this point ; and till we are as well assured of it, as it is possible for us to be, we ought not prodigally to bestow upon him, from equivocal appearances, the precious title of friend. Are we at last convinced that he deserves it, then there must be no reserve; we ought to enter with him into an intercourse of sentiments, of tastes, pleasures and interests.

The next rule, which is not less important, is to choose him only from the society of the good and virtuous. The most long-lived plants are not those that grow the fastest; thus it is with friendship: that is commonly the most firm and durable which grows up but slowly; while that which is hastily contracted is more liable to be dissolved. Lovers of virtue should have none but virtuous men for their friends; and on this point the proof ought principally to turn: because where there is no virtue there is no security that our honour, confidence, and friendship will not be betrayed and abused. In general, they suffer most from pretended friendship who least deserve to suffer. It is very rare for the honest heart to prove distrustful; and more rare still for him not to be deceived, who is a stranger to suspicion. There are men of a character so open, and generous that there is no one but would be a gainer by making them their friends; but, when these contract a friendship they risk more than others : for so many advantages arise from aspiring after their esteem, that they can never be certain that it is not courted with a view to interest : and a self-interested friend is never a true one. It is to those upright and sincere hearts that I especially direct my counsels on friendship, for what matters it if deceivers are deceived?

Though friendship hath nothing in it of a selfish nature, yet it is pleased with kindness and good offices : these are to friends what caresses are to lovers; not reasons for beginning to love, but motives to love more affectionately : like a breath of wind, which, though it produces not the flame, renders it more ardent.

There are so many ways of obliging a friend that in what situation soever we find him, some one of these is always practicable : seize, therefore, every opportunity that offers, and, if it be possible, wait not till he himself tells you in what instance it is in your power to serve him. Endeavour to know his wants, and provide for them before he himself has perceived them; and thus he will always be ready to foresee and prevent

yours. Have a regard however to the delicacy of your friend , for you may perhaps
disoblige through a desire to oblige too much;
cover, therefore, your services with appearances that may seem to dispense with his gratitude. However this be, it is much better to
offend by too much assiduity and bounty
than to confine yourself through avarice , or
want of affection , to barren protestations
of friendship. But would you give your friend
a proof of friendship as strong as it is rare, be
sincere with him in all your discourse : let
the advice you give him , the remonstrances
you make him , be the faithful expressions
of your thoughts and sentiments. Dare to
shew him truth entirely naked : or if through
condescension you adorn her with some
clothing , let it be such as will set off her
beauties without disguising them.

E X A M P L E.

Athens , long after the decline to the Roman empire, still continued the seat of learn-
ing , politeness , and wisdom. Theodoric ,
the Ostrogoth , repaired the schools which
barbarity was suffering to fall into decay ,
and continued those pensions to men of learn-

ing, which avaricious governors had mono-
polized.

In this city, and about this period, Alcander and Septimius were fellow-students
together. The one, the most subtle reasoner
of all the Lyceum; the other, the most elo-
quent speaker in the the academick grove.
al admiration soon begot a friendship.
Their fortunes were nearly equal, and they
were natives of the two most celebrated cities in the world; for Alcander was of
Athens, Septimius came from Rome.

In this state of harmony they lived for
some time together, when Alcander, after
passing the first part of youth in the indo-
lence of philosophy, thought at length of en-
tering into the busy world; and, as a step
previous to this, placed his affections on
Hypatia, a lady of exquisite beauty. The
day of their intended nuptials was fixed;
the previous ceremonies were performed,
and nothing now remained but her being
conducted in triumph to the apartment of
the intended bridegroom.

Alcander's exultation in his own happiness, or being unable to enjoy any satisfaction without making his friend Septimius a
partner, prevailed upon him to introduce

Hypatia to his fellow student; which he
did with all the gaiety of a man who found
himself equally happy in friendship and
love. But this was an interview fatal to the
future peace of both; for Septimius no
sooner saw her, but he was smitten with an
involuntary passion; and, though he used
every effort to suppress desires at once so
imprudent and injust, the emotions of his
mind in a short time became so strong, that
they brought on a fever, which the physicians judged incurable.

During this illness, Alcander watched
him with all the anxiety of fondness, and
brought his mistress to join in those amiable
offices of friendship. The sagacity of the
physicians, by these means, soon discovered
that the cause of their patient's disorder was
love; and Alcander being apprized of their
discovery, at length extorted a confession
from the reluctant dying lover.

It would but delay the narrative to de-
scribe the conflict between love and friendship in the breast of Alcander on this occasion; it is enough to say, that the Athenians
were at that time arrived at such refine-
ment in morals, that every virtue was carried to excess. In short, forgetful of his own
felicity

felicity, he gave up his intended bride, in all her charms, to the young Roman. They were married privately by his connivance, and this unlooked-for change of fortune wrought as unexpected a change in the constitution of the now happy Septimius. In a few days he was perfectly recovered, and ▓▓▓▓t with his fair partner for Rome. Here, by an exertion of those talents which he was so eminently possessed of, Septimius, in a few years, arrived at the highest dignities of the state, and was constituted the city judge, or prætor.

In the mean time, Alcander not only felt the pain of being separated from his friend and his mistress, but a prosecution was also commenced against him by the relations of Hypatia, for having basely given up his bride, as was suggested, for money. His innocence of the crime laid to his charge, and even his eloquence in his own defense, were not able to withstand the influence of a powerful party. He was cast, and condemned to pay an enormous fine. However, being unable to raise so large a sum at the time appointed, his possessions were confiscated, he himself was stripped of the habit of freedom, exposed

L

as a slave in the market — place, and sold to the highest bidder.

A merchant of Thrace becoming his purchaser, Alcander, with some other companions of distress, was carried into that region of desolation and sterility. His stated employment was, to follow the herds of an imperious master; and his success in hunting was all that was allowed him to supply his precarious subsistence. Every morning waked him to a renewal of famine or toil, and every change of season served but to aggravate his unsheltered distress. After some years of bondage, however, an opportunity of escaping offered; he embraced it with ardour; so that, travelling by night, and lodging in caverns by day, to shorten a long story, he at last arrived in Rome. The same day on which Alcander arrived, Septimius sat administering justice in the forum, whither our wanderer came, expecting to be instantly known, and publickly acknowledged by his former friend. Here he stood the whole day amongst the crowd, watching the eyes of the judge, and expecting to be taken notice of; but he was so much altered by a long succession of hardships, that he continued unnoticed amongst the rest; and in the evening, when he was going up to the prætor's chair, he was brutally repulsed by the attending lictors. The attention of the poor is generally driven from one ungrateful object to another; for, night coming on, he now found himself under a necessity of seeking a place to ly in, and yet knew not where to apply. All emaciated, and in rags as he was, none of the citizens would harbour so much wretchedness; and sleeping in the streets might be attended with interruption or danger: in short, he was obliged to take up his lodging in one of the tombs without the city, the usual retreat of guilt, poverty, and despair. In this mansion of horror, laying his head upon an inverted urn, he forgot his miseries for a while in sleep; and found, on his couch, more ease than beds of down can supply to the guilty.

As he continued here, about midnight, two robbers came to make this their retreat; but, happening to disagree about the division of their plunder, one of them stabbed the other to the heart, and left him weltering in blood at the entrance. In these circumstances, he was found next morning dead at the mouth of the vault. This natural ly inducing a farther enquiry, an alarm was spread; the cave was examined; and Alcander was apprehended, and accused of robbery and murder. The circumstances against him were strong, and the wretchedness of his appearance confirmed suspicion. Misfortune and he were now so long acquainted, that he at last became regar⬛⬛⬛ of life. He detested a world where he had found only ingratitude, falshood, and cruelty; he was determined to make no defence; and, thus lowering with resolution, he was dragged, bound with cords, before the tribunal of Septimius. As the proofs were positive against him, and he offered nothing in his own vindication, the judge was proceeding to doom him to a most cruel and ignominious death, when the attention of the multitude was soon divided by another object. The robber, who had been really guilty, was apprehended selling his plunder, and, struck with a panick, had confessed his crime. He was brought bound to the same tribunal, and acquitted every other person of any partnership in his guilt. Alcander's innocence therefore appeared, and the sullen rashness of his conduct remained a wonder to the surrounding multitude ; but their astonishment was still farther increased, when they saw their judge start from his tribunal, to embrace the supposed criminal. Septimius recollected his friend and former benefactor, and hung upon his neck with tears of pity and of joy. Need the sequel be related? Alcander was acquitted ; ▮▮ed the friendship and honours of the principal citizens of Rome ; lived afterwards in happiness and left it to be engraved on his tomb, That no circumstances are so desperate, which Providence may not relieve.

A BYZANTINE HISTORIAN.

GENEROSITY.

SENTIMENTS.

ONE great reason why men practise generosity so little in the world, is their finding so little there : generosity is catching, and if so many men escape it, it is in a great degree, because they meet with no one to give it them.

L 3

How seldom is generosity perfect and pure? How often do men give because it throws a certain inferiority on those who receive and superiority on themselves?

We are generally obliging and serviceable to others, in proportion as they do not want the favour.

True generosity is a duty as indispens necessary as those imposed upon us by law. It is a rule imposed upon us by reason, which should be the sovereign law of a rational being. But this generosity does not consist in obeying every impulse of humanity, in following blind passion for our guide, and in impairing our circumstances by present benefactions which may render us incapable of future ones, or doing justice where it is due.

E X A M P L E.

The conduct of the war against the Falisci being committed to the care of Camillus, the Roman dictator, he besieged Falerii, their capital city, and surrounded it with lines; but at so great a distance from the walls, that there was sufficient room for the besieged to take the air without danger. The Falisci had brought from Greece the custom of committing all their children to the care of one man, who was to instruct them in all the branches of polite litterature, to take them out a walking with him, and see them perform the exercises proper their age. The children had been used often to walk with their master without the walls of the city before the siege; and the fears of an enemy, who kept quiet and at such a distance, were not great enough to make them discontinue their exercise afterwards. But the present school-master proved a traitor. He a first led the youths only along the walls, then he carried them a little farther; and at length, when a favourable opportunity offered, he led them through the guards of the Roman camp, quite to the general's tent. As they were the children of the best families in the place, their treacherous leader, when he came into Camillus's presence, addressed him thus : « With these children I deliver the place you besiege into your hands; they were committed to my care and tuition, but I prefer the friend-ship of Rome to my employment at Falerii ».

Camillus, struck with horror at the treachery, and looking at him with a mena-
cing air : « Traitor, » says he « you do not
address yourself with your impious present
either to a general or a people that resemble you : we have indeed no express and
formal alliance with the Falisci ; but that
which nature has established between
men both does, and shall subsist between us.
War has its rights as well as peace ; and we
have learned to make it with no less justice
than valour. We are in arms, not against
an age which is spared even in cities taken
by assault, but against men armed like
ourselves ; men, who, without any previous injury from us, attacked the Roman
camp at Veii. Thou, to the utmost of thy
power, hast succeeded them by a new and
different kind of crime ; but for me, I shall
conquer, as at Veii, by Roman arts, by
valour, works, and perseverance. »

The traitor was not dismissed with this
reprimand only : Camillus caused him to be
stripped, and to have his hands tied behind
him ; and arming the young scholars with
rods, he ordered them to drive him back
into the city, and to scourge him all the
way, which no doubt they did with a good
will.

At this sight the Falisci , who had been
inconsolable for the loss of their children ,
raised cries of joy : they were charmed
to such a degree , with so uncommon an
example of justice and virtue , that in an
instant they intirely changed their disposition in respect to the Romans , and resolved that moment to have a peace with such
generous enemies. Accordingly they sent
deputies first to the camp , and afterwards
to Rome ; where , when they had audience
of the senate , they addressed themselves to
it in these terms : « Illustrious fathers ,
conquered by you , and your general , in a
manner that can give no offence to gods
and men , we are come to surrender ourselves to you ; and we assure ourselves ;
that we shall live happier under your government , than under our own laws. The
event of this war has brought forth two
excellent examples for mankind. You ;
fathers , have preferred justice to immediate
conquest ; and we , excited by that justice
which we admire , voluntarily present you
the victory.   Liv. lib. v. c. 27.

We see in the famous event which we
have just related the power of virtue , and

what impression it is capable of making upon the mind of man , when solid and sincere. No one can read this fact without feeling himself warmly affected with in- dignation for the perfidious master , who gives up his scholars , and admiration for Camillus , who sends them back to their parents. Sentiments of this kind are free , and do not depend upon the will ; they are implanted in the heart , they are a part of it , and born with us. We must therefore renounce nature , and suppress its voice , to believe , or to say , that virtue and vice are only names without force or reality. It is very evident , in the history of this people , that their reputation for faith to engagements , equity , humanity , and clemency , contributed more than any thing besides to aggrandize the Roman empire.

PLUT. IN CAMILLO. LIV. lib. 5. c. 26.

HAPPINESS

NOT FOUNDED ON WEALTH;

OR,

 ## VICISSITUDES OF HUMAN LIFE.

SENTIMENTS.

You see here a notable instance of the uncertainty of human grandeur, of the mutability of fortune ; let it make a proper impression on you all, but especially on such of you as are in the vigour of your age. Let not present prosperity so far puff up any man as to make him behave with arrogance towards another ; neither let any man confide in his good fortune, for he cannot tell how soon it may forsake him.

It is the lot of mankind to be happy and miserable by turns. Divine wisdom will have it so, and it is exceedingly for our advantage it should be so. By the mediation of this mixture we have the comfort of hope to support us in our distresses, and the apprehensions of a change to keep a check upon us in the very height of our greatness and glory ; so that by this vicissitude of good and evil , we are kept steady in our philosophy , and in our religion. The one puts us in mind of God's omnipotence and justice , the other of his goodness and mercy ; the one tells us that there is no trusting to our strength ; the other preaches faith and resignati the prospect of an over-ruling Providence who takes care of us.

E X A M P L E.

Crœsus was king of Lydia. His very name, which is become a proverb , carries in it an idea of immense riches. The wealth of this prince , to judge of it only by the presents he made to the temple of Delphos, must have been excessively great. Most of those presents were to be seen in the time of Herodotus ; and were worth several millions. We may partly account for the treasures of this prince from certain mines that he had , situate , according to Strabo , between Pergamos and Atarnes ; as also from the little river Pactolus , the sand of which was gold. This uncommon affluence , which is a thing extraordinary , did not enervate or soften the courage

courage of Crœsus. He thought it unworthy of a prince to spend his time in idleness and pleasures. Herodotus observes that he was the first conqueror of the Greeks, who till then had never been subject to a foreign power. But what is still more extraordinary in this prince, though he was immensely rich, and so great a warrior, yet his chief delight was in literature and the sciences. His court was the ordinary residence of those famous and learned men, so revered by antiquity, and distinguished by the name of the seven wise men of Greece. Solon, one of the most celebrated amongst them, after having established new laws at Athens, went to Sardis, where he was received in a manner suitable to the reputation of so great a man. The king, attended with a numerous court, appeared in all his regal pomp and splendor, dressed in the most magnificent apparel, which was all over enriched with gold, and glittered with diamonds. Notwithstanding the novelty of this spectacle to Solon, it did not appear that he was the least moved at it, or that he uttered a word which discovered the least surprise or admiration; on the contrary, people of sense might sufficiently discern from his behaviour,

M

that he looked upon all this outward pomp, as an indication of a little mind, which knows not in what true greatness consists. This coldness and indifference in Solon's first approach gave the king no favourable opinion of his new guest. He afterwards ordered that all his treasures, his magnificent apartments, and costly furniture should shewn him; as if he expected by the multitude of his fine vessels, diamonds, statues, and paintings, to conquer the philosopher's indifference. But it was the king that Solon was come to visit, and not the walls or chambers of his palace. He had no notion of making an estimate of his worth, by these outward appendages, but by himself and personal qualities.

When Solon had seen all, he was brought back to the king: Croesus then asked him, which of mankind, in all his travels, he had found the most truly happy? « One Tellus, » replied Solon, « a citizen of Athens, a very honest and good man, who had lived all his days without indigence, had always seen his country in a flourishing condition, had children that were universally esteemed, with the satisfaction of seeing those children's children, and at last died gloriously fighting for his country. »

Such an answer as this, in which gold and silver were accounted as nothing, seemed to Crœsus to argue a strange ignorance and stupidity. However as he flattered himself with being ranked in the second degree of happiness, he asked him, who of all those he had seen was the next in felicity to Tellus? Solon answered, « Cleobis and Biton of Argos, two brothers, who had left behind them a perfect pattern of fraternal affection, and of the respect due from children to their parents. Upon a solemn festival, when their mother a priestess of Juno, was to go to the temple, the oxen that were so draw her not being ready, the two sons put themselves to the yoke, and drew their mother's chariot thither, which was above five miles distant. All the mothers of the place, ravished with admiration, congratulated the priestess on the piety of her sons. She in the transport of her joy and thankfulness, earnestly intreated the goddess to reward her children with the best thing that heaven could give to man. Her prayers were heard. When the sacrifice was over, her two sons fell asleep in the very temple, and there died in a soft and peaceful slumber. In honour of their piety, the people of Argos consecrated statues to them in the temple of Delphos. » « What ! then , » says Croesus , « you do not reckon me in the number of the happy ? » Solon who was not willing either to flatter or exasperate him , replied calmly; « king of Lydia , besides many other advantages , the gods have given us Grecians a spirit of moderation and reserve , which hath produced amongst us a plain popular kind of philosophy , accompanied with a certain generous freedom , void of pride or ostentation and therefore not well suited to the court of kings. This philosophy , considering what an infinite number of vicissitudes and accidents the life of man is liable to , does not allow us either to glory in any prosperity we enjoy ourselves , or to admire happiness in others, which perhaps may prove only transient or superficial. » From hence he took occasion to observe to him further.» That the life of man seldom exceeds seventy years , which are made up of months , weeks and days , not two of which are exactly alike : so that the time to come is nothing but a series of various accidents which cannot be foreseen. *Therefore* , in our opinion (conti—

nued he) *no man can be esteemed happy, but he whose happiness God continues to the end of his life.* As for others , who are perpetually exposed to a thousand dangers , we account their happiness as uncertain as the crown to a person that is engaged in battle , and has not yet obtained the victory.

It was not long before Croesus experienced the truth of what Solon had told him. He had two sons, one of whom being dumb , was a perpetual subject of affliction to him. The other , named Atys , was distinguished by every good quality , and was his great consolation and delight. One day there was to be an extraordinary hunting-match for the killing of a wild boar which had committed great ravage in the neighbourhood. All the young lords of the court were to be at this hunting. Atys very earnestly importuned his father that he would give him leave to be present. The king granted his request ; but put him under the care of a discreet young prince , who had taken refuge in his court, and was named Adrastus ; and this very Adrastus , as he was aiming his javelin at the boar , unfortunately killed Atys. It was impossible to express either the affliction of the father when he heard of this fatal acci-

M 3

dent, or of the unhappy prince, the innocent author of the murder, who expiated his fault with his blood, stabbing himself in the breast with his own sword, upon the funeral pile of the unfortunate Atys. Two whole years were spent on this occasion in deep mourning, the afflicted father's thoughts being wholly taken up with the loss he ▮▮▮ sustained. But the growing reputation, and great qualities of Cyrus, king of Persia, who then began to make himself known, roused his martial spirits, and diverted his mind to other thoughts. A war commenced between the two kings, in the course of which Cyrus laid siege to Sardis, and carried it; and likewise took Crœsus captive. Crœsus, being a prisoner, was condemned by the conqueror to be burnt alive, with fourteen young Lydians, as a sacrifice and first fruits of his victory. Accordingly the funeral pile was prepared, and that unhappy prince being laid thereon, and just upon the point of execution, recollecting the conversation he formerly had with Solon; was wofully convinced of the truth of that philosopher's admonition; and in remembrance thereof, cried out aloud three times, « O Solon, Solon, Solon! » Cyrus, who with the chief officers of his court, was present at this spectacle, was curious to know why Crœsus pronounced that celebrated philosopher' name with so much vehemence in his extremity. Being told the reason, and reflecting upon the uncertain state of all sublunary things, he was touched with commiseration of the prince's misfortunes, caused him to be taken from the pile, and treated him afterwards as long as he lived, with honour and respect. Thus had Solon the glory with one single sentence to save the life of one king, and give a wholesome lesson of instruction to another.

HEROD. lib. c. 18. — 86 — 91. PLUT. IN SOLON. ROLL. ANT. HIST. vol. ii.

INDUSTRY.

SENTIMENTS.

LOVE labour: if you do not want it for food, you may for physic. He is idle that might be better employed. The idle man is more perplexed what to do than the industrious in doing what he ought. There are but few

who know how to be idle and innocent.
By doing nothing we learn to do ill.

The ordinary manner of spending their
time is the only way of judging of any one's
inclination and genius.

He that follows recreations instead of his
business shall in a little time have no business to follow.

Of all the diversions of life, there is none
so proper to fill up its empty spaces, as the
reading of useful and entertaining authors;
and, with that, the conversation of a well-
chosen friend.

A man of letters never knows the plague
of idleness : when the company of his
friends fail him, he finds a remedy in reading, or in composition.

Action keeps the soul in constant health,
but idleness corrupts and rusts the mind;
for a man of great abilities may, by negli-
gence and idleness, become so mean and
despicable, as to be an incumbrance to
society, and a burden to himself.

E X A M P L E S.

Demosthenes was extremely affected with
the honours which he saw paid to the orator

Callistratus, and still more with his supreme power of eloquence over the minds of men; and not being able to resist its charms, he gave himself wholly up to it; from thenceforth he renounced all other studies and pleasures, and during the continuance of Callistratus at Athens, he never quitted him, but made all the improvement he could from his precepts. The first essay of his eloquence was against his guardians, whom he obliged to refund a part of his fortune. Encouraged by this success, he ventured to speak before the people, but with very ill success. He had a weak voice, a thick way of speaking, and a very short breath; notwithstanding which, his periods were so long, that he was often obliged to stop in the midst of them for respiration. This occasioned his being hissed by the whole audience. As he withdrew, hanging down his head, and in the utmost confusion, Satyrus, one of the most excellent actors of those times, who was his friend, met him; and having learnt from himself the cause of his being so much dejected, he assured him that the evil was not without remedy, and that the case was not so desesperate as he imagined. He desired him to repeat some of the verses of Sophocles or Euripides to him; which he accordingly did. Satyrus spoke them after him, and gave them such graces by the tone, gesture, and spirit, with which he pronounced them, that Demosthenes himself found them quite different from what they were in his own manner of speaking. He perceived plainly what wanted, and applied himself to the acquiring of it.

His efforts to correct his natural defect of utterance, and to perfect himself in pronunciation, of which his friend had made him understand the value, seem almost incredible, and prove that an industrious perseverance can surmount all things. He stammered to such a degree, that he could not pronounce some letters; among others, that with which the name of the art he studied begins; and he was so short-breathed, that he could not utter a whole period without stopping. He overcame these obstacles at length, by putting small pebbles into his mouth; and pronouncing several verses in that manner without interruption, and with walking and going up steep and difficult places, so that at last no letter made him hesitate, and

his breath held out through the longest periods. He went also to the sea — side and
whilst the waves were in the most violent
agitation , he pronounced harangues , to ac-
custom himself , by the confused noise of
the waters , to the roar of the people ,
and the tumultuous cries of public assemblies.

Demosthenes took no less care of his action
than his voice. He had a large looking-glass
in his house which served to teach him
gesture , and at which he used to declaim ,
before he spoke in public. To correct a fault ,
which he had contracted by an ill habit of
shrugging up his shoulders , he practised
standing upright in a kind of very narrow
pulpit , or rostrum , over which hung a
halbert in such a manner , that if in the
heat of the action that motion escaped
him , the point of the weapon might serve
at the same time to admonish and correct him.

His application to study was no less surprising. To be the more removed from noise,
and less subject to distraction , he caused a
small room to be made for him under ground,
in which he shut himself up sometimes for
whole months , shaving on purpose half his
head and face , that he might not be in

a condition to go abroad. It was there by
the light of a small lamp he composed the
admirable orations , which were said by
those who envied him to smell of the oil ,
to imply that they were too elaborate, « It is
plain , » replied he , « yours did not cost you
so much trouble. » He rose very early in the
morning , and used to say , that he
sorry when any workman was at his business before him. We may farther judge of
his extraordinary efforts to acquire an ex-
cellence of every kind, from the pains he
took in copying Thucydide's History eight
times with his own hand, in order to render
the style of that great man familiar to him.

His pains were well bestowed ; for it was
by these means that he carried the art of de-
claiming to the highest degree of perfection
of which it was capable ; whence , it is
plain , he well knew its value and importance. When he was asked three several
times which quality he thought most necessary in an orator , he gave no other answer
than «Pronunciation ;» insinuating, by making
the reply three times successively , that
qualification to be the only one of which the
want could least be concealed , and which
was the most capable of concealing other
defects ;

defects ; and that pronunciation alone could give considerable weight even to an indifferent orator , when, without it, the most excellent could not hope the least success. As to Demosthenes , Cicero tells us , that his success was so great , that all Greece came in crowds to Athens to hear him speak ; and he adds , that merit so great as his could not but have the desired effect.

Lysander , the famous Lacedemonian general , having brought magnificent presents to Cyrus , the younger son of Darius , king of Persia ; that young prince , who piqued himself more upon his integrity and politeness than nobility and grandeur , pleased himself with conducting in person so illustrious a guest through his gardens , and making him observe the various beauties of them. Lysander , struck with so fine a prospect , admired the manner in which the several parts were laid out ; the height and projection of the trees ; the neatness and disposition of the walks ; the abundance of fruits , planted with an art which had known how to unite the useful with the agreeable ; the beauty of the parterres , and the glowing variety of flowers , exhaling odours univer-

N

sally throughout the delightful scene. « Every
thing charms and transports me in this
place , » said Lysander , addressing himself
to Cyrus ; « but what strikes me most is the
exquisite taste , and elegant industry of the
person , who drew the plan of the several
parts of this garden , and gave it the fine
order , wonderful disposition , and happiness of symmetry , which I cannot sufficiently admire. Cyrus, infinitely pleased with
this discourse , replied , « It was I who
drew the plan , and intirely marked it out ;
and not only that , many of the trees which
you see were planted with my own hands. »
« What ! » replied Lysander , viewing him
from head to foot , is it possible , with these
purple robes and splendid vestments , those
strings of jewels and bracelets of gold, those
buskins so richly embroidered , that you
could play the gardener , and employ your
royal hand in planting trees ? » « Does that
surprise you ? » said Cyrus : « I protest with
the utmost sincerity ; that when my health
admits , I never sit down to table without
having made myself sweat with some fatigue
or other , either in military exercise , rural
labour , or some other toilsome employment ,
to which I apply with pleasure , and without

sparing myself. » Lysander was amazed at this discourse, and pressing him by the hand, « Cyrus, » said he, « you are truly happy, and deserve your high fortune, because you unite it with virtue. »

CIC. DE SENECT. 39.

INGRATITUDE.

SENTIMENTS.

INGRATITUDE is a crime so shameful, that there never was a man found who would own himself guilty of it.

The ungrateful are neither fit to serve the gods, their country, nor their friends.

Ingratitude perverts all the measures of religion and society, by making it dangerous to be charitable and good natured : however, it is better to expose ourselves to ingratitude than to be wanting to the distressed.

The pleasure a man of honour enjoys in the consciousness of having performed his duty, is a reward he pays himself for all his pains. Applause, esteem, and acknowledgments, as they are not always paid him, so are they but of little account with him.

N 2

E X A M P L E S.

A Macedonian soldier had in many instances distinguished himself by extraordinary acts of valour, and had received many marks of Philip's favour and approbation. On some occasion he embarked on board a vessel, which was wrecked by a violent storm, and he himself cast on shore, helpless, naked, and scarcely with the appearance of life. One of the same country, whose lands lay contiguous to the sea, came opportunely to be witness of his distress, and, with the utmost humanity and concern, flew to the relief of the unhappy stranger. He bore him to his house, laid him in his own bed, revived, cherished, and for forty days supplied him freely with all the necessaries and conveniencies which his languishing condition could require. The soldier, thus happily rescued from death, was incessant in the warmest expressions of gratitude to his benefactor; assured him of his interest with the king, and of his power and resolution of obtaining for him, from the royal bounty, the noble return which such extraordinary benevolence had merited. He was now completely recovered, and his kind host supplied him with money to pursue his journey. Some time after he presented himself before the king; he recounted his misfortunes and magnified his services; and this inhuman wretch, who had looked with an eye of envy on the possessions of the man who had preserved his life, was now so abandoned to all sense of gratitude, as to request that the king would bestow upon him the house and lands where he had been so kindly and tenderly entertained. Unhappily Philip, without examination, inconsiderately and precipitately granted his infamous request; and this soldier now returned to his preserver, and repaid his goodness, by driving him from his settlement, and taking immediate possession of all the fruits of his honest industry. The poor man, stung with this instance of unparalleled ingratitude and insensibility, boldly determined, instead of submitting to his wrong, to seek relief, and, in a letter addressed to Philip, represented his own and the soldier's conduct in a lively and affecting manner. The king was fired with indignation, and ordered justice should be instantly done; that the possessions should be immediately restored to the man whose charitable offices had been thus

horridly repaid ; and having seized his soldier, caused these words to be branded on
his forehead, « The ungrateful guest; » a
character infamous in every age, and among
all nations ; but particularly among the
Græks, who from the earliest times, were
most jealously observant of the laws of hos-
pitality.

Xenocrates was a very eminent philosopher, the disciple and successor of Plato,
alike remarkable for his wisdom in words,
and for the probity of his actions. He was
likewise a great writer; for we have the
titles of above sixty treatises which he composed. His disinterestedness and love of his
country was very remarkable, and the services he had done it very great. Being sent
ambassador to Antipater in Macedonia, to
intreat him to set at liberty some Athenian
prisoners, on his arrival, before he had his
audience, Antipater invited him to an entertainment. Xenocrates answered him in
these verses of Homer, spoken by Ulysses to
Circe, when she pressed him to eat of the
dainties set before him :

» Ill fits it me, whose friends are sunk to beasts,
» To quaff thy bowls, or riot in thy feasts.

» Me wouldst thou please, for them thy cares employ,
» And them to me restore , and me to joy. »

Antipater was so well pleased with his
presence of mind , and happy application of
these verses , that without more ado , he
set the Athenians free. But notwithstanding
this , and many other advantages his country
reaped from his wisdom and virtue , he was
suffered to grow so poor as not to be able to
pay his tribute ; and then . with shameless
ingratitude , the Athenians condemned him
to be sold for a slave , which was accordingly done. But Demetrius the Phalerian
bought and restored him to his liberty , pay-
ing his price into the public treasury.

JUSTICE.

SENTIMENTS.

JUSTICE in the general acceptation of the
word , is that virtue by which we render to
God , our neighbour , and ourselves , that
which is their due. It comprehends all our
duties ; and to be just , and to be virtuous , is
the same thing. But we shall here consider

justice only as a principle of equity which causes a rectitude of conduct , and excites us to render our species what in particular is due to it from every individual.

Of all the virtues justice is the best ;
Valour without it is a common pest,
Pirates and thieves, too oft with courage grac'd,
Shew us how ill that virtue may be plac'd.
'Tis our complexion makes us chaste and brave;
Justice from reason and from heaven we have ;
All other virtues dwell but in the blood ;
This in the soul , and gives the name of good.

EXAMPLE.

Among the several virtues of Aristides, that for which he was most renowned was justice ; because this virtue is of most general use , its benefits extending to a greater number of persons , as it is the foundation , and in a manner , the soul of every public office and employment. Hence it was that Aristides , though in low circumstances , and of mean extraction , obtained the glorious surname of the Just ; a title , says Plutarch, truly royal , or rather truly divine : but of which princes are seldom ambitious , because generally ignorant of its beauty and excellency. They choose rather to be called , the

Conquerors of Cities , and the Thunderbolts of War , preferring the vain honour of pompous titles , which convey no other idea than violence and slaughter, to the solid glory of those expressive of goodness and virtue. How much Aristides deserved the title given him , will appear in the following instances , though it ought to be observed , that he acquired it not by one or two particular actions, but by the whole tenor of his conduct.

Themistocles having conceived the design of supplanting the Lacedemonians , and of taking the government of Greece out of their hands, in order to put it into those of the Athenians ; kept his eye and his thoughts continually fixed upon that great project : and as he was not very nice or scrupulous in the choice of his measures , whatever tended towards the accomplishing' of the end he had in view , he looked upon as just and lawful.

On a certain day then he declared in a full assembly of the people , that he had a very important design to propose ; but that he could not communicate it to the people , because its success required it should be carried on with the greatest secrecy; he therefore desired they would appoint a person

to whom he might explain himself upon the
matter in question. Aristides was unanimously fixed upon by the whole assembly,
who referred themselves intirely to his
opinion of the affair ; so great a confidence
had they both in his probity and prudence.
Themistocles , therefore , having taken him
aside , told him that the design he had conceived was to burn the fleet belonging to
the rest of the Grecian states , which then
lay in a neighbouring port; and by this means
Athens would certainly become mistress of all
Greece. Aristides hereupon returned to the
assembly : and only declared to them that
indeed nothing could be more advantageous
to the commonwealth than Themistocles's
project ; but that at the same time nothing
in the world could be more unjust. All the
people unanimously ordained that Themistocles should entirely desist from his project.

I do not know whether all history can
afford us a fact more worthy of admiration
than this. It is not a company of philosophers
(to whom it costs nothing to establish fine
maxims and sublime notions of morality in
the schools) who determine on this occasion that the consideration of profit and ad—

vantage ought never to prevail in preference to what is honest and just ; but the whole people who are highly interested in the proposal made to them , that are convinced it is of the greatest importance to the welfare of the state , and who , however , reject it with unanimous consent , and without a moment's hesitation ; and for this only reason that it is contrary to justice. How black and perfidious , on the other hand , was the design which Themistocles proposed to them , of burning the fleet of their Grecian confederates , at a time of entire peace , solely to aggrandize the power of the Athenians ! Had he an hundred times the merit ascribed to him , this single action would be sufficient to sully all his glory : for it is the heart , that is to say , integrity and probity , that constitutes and distinguishes true merit.

PLUT. IN THEMIST. — IN ARIST.

L U X U R Y.

S E N T I M E N T S.

THAT which is splendor, sumptuousness
and magnificence in people of quality, is
in private men extravagance, folly, and
impertinence.

It is a sure and ancient maxim in politics,
That to humour the people, in enervat-
ing themselves with expensive pleasures and
feasts, shows and luxury, pomp and delicacy; to alienate them from what is solid
and praise-worthy; and contrive baits for
their depraved fancies, is to make the greatest advances to a despotic power.

If sensuality were pleasure, beasts are
happier than men. Pleasures unduly taken
enervate the soul, make fools of the wise,
and cowards of the brave. A libertine life
is not a life of liberty.

So stupid and brutish, so worthless and
scandalous, are too many seen in this degenerate age, that grandeur and equipage are
looked upon as more indispensable than cha-
rity; and those creatures which contribute
merely

merely to our pomp, or our diversion, are
more tenderly and sumptuously maintained,
than such as are in necessity among ourselves.

Pray what were you made for? (says the
emperor Aurelius) for your pleasures! Common sense will not bear so scandalous an
answer.

The declension of manners in any state is
always attended with that of empire and dominion.

E X A M P L E.

What made the Persian troops in Cyrus's
time looked upon to be invincible, was the
temperate and hard life to which they were
accustomed from their infancy. Add to this
the influence of the prince's example, who
made it his ambition to surpass all his subjects in regularity, was the most abstemious,
and sober in his manner of life, as plain in his
dress and as much inured to hardships and fatigue, as any of his subjects, and the bravest
and most intrepid in the time of action. What
might not be expected from a people so
formed and so trained up? By them it was
that Cyrus conquered a great part of the
world. After all his victories he continued to
exhort his army and people not to degenerate
O

from their ancient virtue , that they might
not eclipse the glory they had acquired ; but
carefully preserve that simplicity , sobriety,
temperance , and love of labour which were
the means by which they had obtained it.
But , alas , it was not long ere Cyrus himself sowed the first seeds of that luxury
which soon overspread and corrupted the
whole nation : for being to shew himself in
a particular occasion to his new conquered
subjects , he thought proper , in order to
heighten the splendor of his regal dignity , to
make a pompous display of all the magnificence and shew that could be contrived to
dazzle the eyes of the people. Among other
things he changed his own apparel , as also
that of his officers, giving them all garments
richly shining with gold and purple , instead
of their Persian clothes , which were plain
and simple. To be all of a piece , the plain
and decent furniture of his palace was ex-
changed for vessels of gold and silver without number , and then the most exquisite
meats, the rarest birds, and the costliest
dainties were procured , though not without
an immense expence , from the most distant
places. It must be acknowledged that the
rank of kings requires a suitable grandeur

and magnificence , which may on certain
occasions be carried even to a degree of
pomp and splendor : but princes possessed
of real and solid merit, have a thousand ways
of making up what they may seem to lose ,
by retrenching some part of their outward
state and magnificence. Cyrus himself had
_und by experience , that a king is more
sure of gaining respect from his people by
the wisdom of his conduct , than by the
greatness of his expences ; and that affection
and confidence produce a closer attachment
to his person , than a vain admiration of unnecessary pomp and grandeur. Be that as it
will, Cyrus's last example became very con-
tagious ; his courtiers , his generals and officers first caught the infection , and in time
carried their extravagance and luxury to such
an excess as was little better than downright
madness. This taste for vanity and expence
having first prevailed at court , soon spread
itself into the cities and provinces , and in a
little time infected the whole nation , and
was one of the principal causes of the ruin
of that empire which Cyrus himself had
founded.

What is here said of the fatal effect of
luxury is not peculiar to the Persian empire.

O 2

The most judicious historians, the most learned philosophers , and the profoundest politicians , all lay it down as a certain indisputable maxim , that wherever luxury prevails, it never fails to destroy the most flourishing states and kingdoms ; and the experience of all ages and nations does but too clearly demonstrate this maxim.

Ancient authors seem to have strove who should most extol the innocence of manners that reigned amongst the Scythians by magnificent encomiums.

Homer in particular, whose opinion ought to be of great weight, calls them, *The most just and upright of men.*

That of Horace(1) I shall transcribe at large. The poet does not confine it entirely to them, but joins the Getæ with their near neighbours. It is in that beautiful ode where he

---

(1) Campestres melius Scythæ
(Quorum plaustra vagas ritè trahunt domos)
Vivunt et rigidi Getæ ;
Immetata quibus jugera liberas
Fruges et cererem ferunt ;
Nec cultura placet longior annuâ :
Defunctumque laboribus
Æquali recreet sorte vicarius.
Illic matre carentibus
Privignis mulier temperat innocens :

inveighs against the luxury and irregulari-
ties of the age he lived in. After having told
us that peace and tranquillity of mind is
not to be procured either by immense riches
or sumptuous buildings, he adds, « An
hundred times happier are the Scythians,
who roam about in their itinerant houses,
their waggons; and happier even are the
frozen Getæ. With them the earth without
being divided by land-mark, produceth her
fruits, which are gathered in common. There
each man's tillage is but of one year's continuance; and when that term of his labour is
expired, he is relieved by a successor, who
takes his place, and manures the ground on
the same conditions. There the innocent
step-mother forms no cruel designs against
the lives of their husband's children by a
former wife. The wives do not pretend to do-
mineer over their husbands on account of
their fortunes, nor are they to be corrupted
by the insinuating language of spruce adulte-

Nec dotata regit virum
Conjux, nec nitido fidit adulteros
    Dos est magna, parentium
Virtus, et metuens alterius viri
    Certo fœdere castitas;
Et peccare nefas, aut pretium est mori.
                    Hor. l. iii. Od. 24.
                        O 3

rers. The greatest portion of the maiden , is her father and mother's virtue , her inviolable attachment to her husband , and her perfect disregard to all other men. They dare not be unfaithful, because they are convinced that infidelity is a crime , and its reward is death. »

Justin finishes his character of the Scythians with a very judicious reflection : « It is a surprising thing , says he , that an happy natural disposition , without the assistance of education , should carry the Scythians to such a degree of wisdom and moderation, as the Grecians could not attain to , neither by the institutions of their legislators , nor the rules and precepts of all their philosophers ; and that the manners of a barbarous nation should be preferable to those of a people so much improved and refined by the polite arts and sciences : so much more effectual and advantageous was the ignorance of vice in the one , to the knowledge of virtue in the other ! »

When we consider the manners and character of the Scythians , without prejudice , can we possibly forbear to look upon them with esteem and admiration ? Does not their manner of living, as to the exterior part of it at least , bear a great ressemblance to that of the patriarchs , who had no fixed habitation , who had no other occupation than that of feeding their flocks and herds, and who dwelt in tents ? Can we believe this people were much to be pitied for not understanding , or rather for despising the use of gold and silver ? Is it not to be wished , that those metals had for ever lain buried in the bowels of the earth , and that they had never been dug from thence to become the causes and instruments of all vices and iniquity ? Were those nations that had them in the greatest plenty , more healthful or robust than the Scythians ? Did they live to a greater age than they ? or did they spend their lives in greater freedom and tranquillity, or a greater exemption from cares and trouble ? Quite the reverse. Let us acknowledge it, to the shame of ancient philosophy ; the Scythians , who did not particularly apply themselves to the study of wisdom , carried it however to a greater height in their practice , than either the Egyptians , Grecians , or any other civilized nations. They did not give the name of goods , or riches to any thing , but what , in a human way of speaking , truly deserved that title , as health , strength , courage , the love of labour and liberty , innocence of life , sincerity, an abhorrence of all fraud and dissimulation; in a word, all such qualities as render a man more virtuous and more valuable.

But at length (who could believe it ?) luxury, that might be thought only to thrive in an agreeable and delightful soil penetrated into this rough and uncultivated region and breaking down the fences which the constant practice of several ages founded in the nature of the climate, and the genius of the people had set against it, did at last effectually corrupt the manners of the Scythians, and bring them, in that respect, upon a level with other nations where it had long been predominant. Is is Strabo that acquaints us with this particular, which is well worth our notice; he lived in the time of Augustus and Tiberius : after he had greatly commended the simplicity, frugality, and innocence of the ancient Scythians, and their extreme aversion to all dissimulation and deceit, he owns that their intercourse in later times with other nations had extirpated those virtues, and planted the contrary vices in their stead. « One would think, » says he, « that the natural effect of such an intercourse with civilized and polite nations should have consisted only in rendering them more humanized and courteous , by softening that air of savageness and ferocity which they had before ; but instead of that , it introduced a total dissolution of manners amongst them , and quite transformed them into different creatures.» It is undoubtedly in reference to this change , that Athenæus says , « the Scythians abandoned themselves to voluptuousness and luxury, at the same time that they suffered self-interest and avarice to prevail amongst them. » Strabo , in making the remark above-mentioned , does not deny but that it was to the Romans and Grecians this fatal change of manners was owing. « Our example , » says he , « has perverted almost all the nations of the world : by carrying the refinements of luxury and pleasures amongst them , we have taught them insincerity and fraud , and a thousand kinds of shameful and infamous arts to get money.» It is a miserable talent, and a very unhappy distinction , for a nation through its ingenuity of inventing modes and refining upon every thing that tends to nourish and promote luxury , to become the corrupter of all its neighbours , and the author , as it were , of their vices and debauchery. To these vices succeeded a softness and effeminacy which rendered them an easy prey to enemies.

STRABO l. vii. p. 3o1. JUST. l. ii. c. 2. ATHEN. l. xii. p. 524. ROLL. ANT. HIST. vol. 3. 147.

MAGISTRATE.

SENTIMENTS.

THE judge, in giving his suffrage, ought not to consider himself as alone, nor that he is at liberty to pronounce according to his own inclinations; but to represent to himself that he has around him, law, religion, equity, integrity, and fidelity, which form his council, and ought to dictate his words.

In the same manner as the people are subservient to the magistrates, magistrates are subservient to the laws; and it may be truly said, that the magistrate is a speaking law, and the law a mute magistrate.

Titles of honour conferred on such as have no personal merit, are at best but the royal stamp set upon base metal.

It is not the place that maketh the person ,
but the person that maketh the place honourable.

The world is a theatre ; the best actors are
those that represent their parts most naturally;
but the wisest are seldom the heroes of the
play. It is not to be considered who is prince,
or who is peasant ; but who acts the prince ,
or the peasant best.

EXAMPLE.

The young people of Athens , dazzled
with the glory of Themistocles, Cimon, and
Pericles , and full of a wild ambition , after
having received , for some time , the lessons
of the Sophists, who promised to make them
great politicians , conceived themselves capable of every thing, and aspired at the highest employments. One of these , named
Glauco, had taken it so strongly into his head
to enter upon the administration of public affairs , that none of his friends were able to
divert him from a design so little consistent
with his age and capacity. Socrates , meeting
him one day , very genteelly engaged him in
a conversation upon the subject. « You are
desirous then of a share in the government of

the republic ? » said Socrates. « True , »
replied Glauco. « You cannot have a more
honourable design , answered Socrates ;
for if you succeed you will have it in your
power to serve your friends effectually , to
aggrandize your family , and to extend the
confines of your country. You will make
yourself known not only to Athens , but
throughout all Greece ; and perhaps your
renown , like that of Themistocles , may
spread abroad among the barbarous nations.»
So smooth and insinuating a prelude was
extremely pleasing to the young man. He
staid willingly , and the conversation continued. Since you desire to be esteemed and
honoured , no doubt your view is to be
useful to the public ? » « Certainly. » « Tell
me then , I beseech you , in the name of
the gods , what is the first service you propose to render to the state ? » As Glauco
seemed at a loss , and meditated upon what
he should answer , « I presume , » continued
Socrates , « it is to enrich it , that is to say ,
to augment its revenues. » « My very
thought. » « You are well versed then undoubtedly , in the revenues of the state , and
know perfectly to what they amount ; you
have not failed to make them your particular

lar study ; in order that if a fund should happen to fail by any unforeseen accident, you might be able to supply the deficiency by another » « I protest, « replied Glauco, « that never entered into my thoughts. » « At least you will tell me to what the expences of the republic amount ; for you must know the importance of retrenching such as are superfluous.» « I own, says Glauco, » I am as little informed in this point as the other. » « You must therefore refer your design of enriching the state to another time, for it is impossible you should do it whilst you are unacquainted with its revenues and expences. » « But, » said Glauco, « there is still another means which you have not mentioned ; a state may be enriched by the ruin of its enemies. » « You are in the right, » replied Socrates ; « but that depends upon its being the strongest, otherwise it incurs the danger of losing what it has. For which reason, he who talks of engaging in a war, ought to know the forces on both sides ; that if he finds his own party strongest, he may boldly advise the war, and if weakest, dissuade the people from undertaking it. Now do you know the strength of our republic ; and that of our enemies, by sea and land ?

P

Have you a state of them in writing ? Be so kind as to let me see it. » « I have it not at present », said Glauco. « I see then, » said Socrates, « that we shall not presently enter into a war, if you are charged with the government : for you have abundance of enquiries to make, and much pains to go through, *before you will resolve upon it.* »

He ran over several other articles no less important, with which Glauco was equally unacquainted, till he brought him to confess how ridiculous those people were who have the rashness to intrude into government, without any other preparation for the service of the public, than that of an high esteem for themselves and an immoderate ambition of rising to the first places and dignities. «Have a care, dear Glauco, » said Socrates, « lest a too warm desire of honours should deceive you into pursuits that may cover you with shame, by setting your incapacity and slender abilities in full light » Glauco improved from the wise admonitions of Socrates, and took time to inform himself in private before he ventured to appear in public. This is a lesson for all ages, and may be very useful to persons in all stations and conditions in life.

MAGNANIMITY.

SENTIMENTS.

MAGNANIMITY is sufficiently defined by its name ; yet we may say of it , that it is the good sense of pride , and the noblest way of acquiring applause. It renders the soul superior to the trouble, disorder , and emotion which the appearance of great danger might excite ; and it is by this quality that heroes maintain their tranquillity, and preserve the free use of their reason in the most surprising and dreadful accidents.

It admires the same quality in its enemy; and fame , glory , conquests , desire of opportunities to pardon and oblige their opposers , are what glow in the minds of the brave. Magnanimity and courage are inseparable.

EXAMPLES.

The inhabitants of Privernum being subdued and taken prisoners after a revolt , one

P 2

of them being asked by a Roman senator, who was for putting them all to death, what punishment he and his fellow captives deserved, answered with great intrepidity, « We deserve that punishment which is due to men who are jealous of their liberty, and think themselves worthy of it. » Plautinus perceiving that his answer exasperated some of the senators, endeavoured to prevent the ill effects of it, by putting a milder question to the prisoners : « How would you behave, » says he, « if Rome should pardon you ? » « Our conduct, » replied the generous captive, « depends upon yours. If the peace you grant be an honourable one, you may depend on a constant fidelity on our parts : if the terms of it be hard and dishonourable, lay no stress on our adherence to you. » Some of the judges construed these words as menaces; but the wiser part finding in them a great deal of magnanimity, cried out, that a nation whose only desire was liberty, and their only fear that of losing it, was worthy to become Roman. Accordingly a decree passed in favour of the prisoners, and Privernum was declared a municipium. Thus the bold sincerity of one man saved his country , and gained it the privilege of being in-corporated into the Roman state.

LIV. lib. viii. c. 20 , 21.

Alexander the Great , having totally de-feated the numerous army of Porus , an In-dian prince of great courage and prudence, desired to see him. After much intreaty , Porus consented , and accordingly set for-ward. Alexander who had been told of his coming, advanced forward in order to receive him , with some of his train. Being come pretty near , Alexander stopped , purposely, to take a view of his stature and noble mien, he being much above the common height. Porus did not seem dejected at his misfortune, but came up with a resolute countenance , like a valiant warrior , whose courage in de-fending his dominions ought to acquire the esteem of the brave Prince who had taken him prisoner. Alexander spoke first , and with an august and gracious air asked him , « How he desired to be treated ? » « Like a king , » replied Porus. « But » continued Alexander , « do you ask nothing more ? » « No, » replied Porus , « all things are in-cluded in that single word. » Alexander , struck with this greatness of soul , the mag-

P 3

nanimity of which seemed heightened by distress , did not only restore him his king—dom , but annexed other provinces to it , and treated him with the highest testimonies of honour , esteem and friendship. Porus was faithful to him till his death. It is hard to say , whether the victor or the vanquished best *deserved* praise on this occasion.

PATIENCE.

SENTIMENTS.

The evils by which life is embittered may be reduced to these four. 1 Natural evils ; or those to which we are by nature subject as men , and as perishable animals. The great—est of these are , the death of those whom we love , and of ourselves. 2. Those from which we might be exempted by a virtuous and prudent conduct , but which are the in—separable consequences of imprudence or vice , which we shall call punishments; as infamy proceeding from fraud , poverty from prodigality , debility and disease from intem—perance. 3. Those by which the fortitude of the good is exercised, such as the persecutions raised against them by the wicked. To these may be added, 4. The opposition against which we must perpetually struggle, arising from the diversity of sentiments, manners, and characters of the persons among whom we live.

Under all these evils patience is not only necessary but useful ; it is necessary, because the laws of nature have made it a duty, and to murmur against natural events is to affront Providence ; it is useful, because it renders our sufferings lighter, shorter, and less dangerous.

A virtuous and well-disposed person is like to good metal ; the more he is fired, the more he is refined, the more he is opposed, the more he is approved : wrongs may well try him and touch him, but cannot imprint in him any false stamp.

The man therefore who possesses this virtue, (patience), in this ample sense of it, stands upon an eminence, and sees human things below him ; the tempest indeed may reach him, but he stands secure and collected against it upon the basis of conscious virtue, which the severest storm can seldom shake, and never overthrow.

Resign'd in ev'ry state
With patience bear , with prudence push your fate!
By suffering well our fortune we subdue ,
Fly when she frowns, and when she calls pursue.

E X A M P L E S.

Tiberius, the Roman emperor, at the beginning of his reign , acted in most things
like a truly generous , good-natured , and
clement prince. All slanderous reports, libels
and lampoons upon him and his administration , he bore with extraordinary patience, saying , « That in a free state the
thoughts and tongues of every man ought to
be free : » and when the senate would have
proceeded against some who had published
libels against him , he would not consent to
it , saying , « We have not time enough to
attend to such trifles : if you once open a
door to such informations , you will be able
to do nothing else ; for under that pretence ,
every man will revenge himself upon his
enemy by accusing him to you. » Being informed , that one had spoken detractingly
of him : « If he speaks ill of me, » says he,
« I will give him as good an account of my
words and actions as I can ; and if that is
not sufficient , I will satisfy myself with

having as bad an opinion of him as he has of me. » Thus far even Tiberius may be an example to others.

Of all the philosophers which the sect of the Stoics ever produced, Epitectus is by far the most renowned. He is supposed to have been a native of Hierapolis in Phrygia, was for some time a slave, and belonged to Epaphroditus, one of Nero's life-guards. He reduced all his philosophy to two points only, viz. « To suffer evils with patience, and enjoy pleasures with moderation ; » which he expressed with these celebrated words ; bear and forbear. Of the former he gave a memorable example. As his master was one day squeezing his leg, in order to torment him, Epitectus said to him very calmly ; « You will break my leg ; » which happening accordingly ; « did not I tell you, » said he, smiling, « that you would break my leg ? » ORIG. IN CELS. l. vii. SUID. p. 996.

One of the most distinguishing qualities of Socrates, was a tranquillity of soul, that no accident, no loss, no injury, no ill treatment, could ever alter. Some have believed that he was by nature hasty and passionate, and that the moderation to which he had attained, was the effect of his reflections and endeavours to subdue and correct himself; which would still add to his merit.

Seneca tells us, that he had desired his friends to apprize him whenever they saw him ready to fall into a passion, and had given them that privilege over him which he took himself with them. Indeed the best time to call in aid against rage and anger that have so violent and sudden a power over us, is when we are yet ourselves, and in cool blood. At the first signal, the least animadversion, he either softened his tone or was silent. Finding himself in great emotion against a slave, « I would beat you, » says he, « if I were not angry. » Having received a box on the ear, he contented himself, by only saying with a smile, « It is a misfortune not to know when to put on a helmet. » Socrates meeting a gentleman of rank in the street, saluted him, but the gentleman took no notice of it. His friends in company, observing what passed, told the philosopher, « that they were so exasperated at the man's incivility, they had a good mind to resent it. » But he very calmly made answer, « If you meet any person on the road in a worse habit of body than yourself, would you think that you had reason to be enraged at him on that account ? if not, pray then, what greater reason can you have for being incensed at a man of a worse habit of mind than any of yourselves ? » But without going out of his house, he found enough to exercise his patience in all its extent. Xantippe, his wife, put it to the severest proofs, by her captious, passionate, violent disposition. Never was woman of so furious and fantastical a spirit, and so bad a temper. There was no kind of abuse or injurious treatment which he had not to experience from her. She was once so transported with rage against him, that she tore off his cloak in the open street. Whereupon his friends told him, that such treatment was insufferable, and that he ought to give her a severe drubbing for it, « Yes, a fine piece of sport indeed, » says he, « while she and I were buffeting one another, you in your turns, I suppose, would animate us on to the combat ; while one cried out, Well done Socrates, another would say, Well hit Xantippe. At another time, having vented all the reproaches her fury could suggest, he went out and sat before the door. His calm and unconcerned behaviour did but irritate her so much the more, and in the excess of her rage, she ran up stairs and emptied the —— pot upon his head; at which he only laughed, and said, «That so much thunder must needs produce a shower.» Alcibiades, his friend talking with him one day about his wife, told him, he wondered how he could bear such an everlasting scold in the same house with him? he replied, « I have so accustomed myself to expect it, that it now offends me no more than the noise of the carriages in the streets.» The same disposition of mind was visible in other respects, and continued with him to his last moments. When he was told, that the Athenians had condemned him to die, he replied, without the least emotion, « and Nature them.»Apollodorus,one of his friends and disciples, having expressed his grief for his dying innocent, « What, » replied he, with a smile, « would you have had me die guilty? »

This sentence did no shake the constancy of Socrates in the least. «I am going », says he, addressing himself to his judges with a noble tranquillity, « to suffer death by your order, to which nature had condemned me from the first moment of my birth; but my

accusers

accusers will suffer no less from infamy and injustice by the decrees of truth. » When the deadly potion was brought him , he drank it off with an amazing fortitude and a serenity of aspect not to be expressed or even conceived. — Till then his friends , with great violence to themselves , had refrained from tears ; but after he had drank the poison , they were no longer their own masters , but wept abundantly. Apollodorus , who had been in tears for some time , began to lament with such excessive grief, as pierced the hearts of all that were present. Socrates alone remained unmoved , and even reproved his friends , though with his usual mildness and good nature. What are you doing , » said he to them , « I admire at you. Ah ! what is become of your virtue ? was it not for this I sent away the women , that they might not fall into these weaknesses ; for I have always heard say that we ought to die peaceably and blessing the gods ? Be at ease , I beg of you , and shew more constancy and resolution. Thus died Socrates , the wisest and the best man the heathen world could ever boast of.

Q

PATRIOTISM,

OR,

LOVE OF ONE'S COUNTRY. ◀

SENTIMENTS.

LOVE of our country is one of the noblest passions that can warm and animate the human breast. It includes all the limited and particular affections to our parents, children, friends, neighbours, fellow-citizens, and countrymen. It ought to direct and limit their more confined and partial actions within their proper and natural bounds, and never let them encroach on those sacred and first regards we owe to the great public to which we belong. Were we solitary creatures detached from the rest of mankind, and without any capacity of comprehending a public interest, or without affections leading us to desire and pursue it, it would not be our duty to mind it, nor criminal to neglect it. But as we are parts of the public system, and are not only capable of taking in large views of its interests, but by the strongest affections connected with it, and prompted to take a share of its concerns, we are under the most sacred ties to prosecute its security and welfare with the utmost ardor, especially in times of public trial.

E X A M P L E S.

So deeply was the love of his country impressed on the mind of Alexander, the Roman emperor, that he is said never to have given any public office out of favour or friendship; but to have employed such only, as were both by himself and the senate judged the best qualified for the discharge of the trust reposed in them. He preferred one to the command of the guards, who had retired into the country on purpose to avoid that office, saying, that with him the declining such honourable employments was the best recommendation to them. He would not suffer any important employments to be sold, saying, « He who buys must sell in his turn; and it would be unjust to punish one for selling, after he has been suffered to buy. » He never pardoned any crime committed against the public; but suffered no one to be

Q 2

condemned till his cause was thoroughly heard , and his offence evidently proved. He was an irreconcilable enemy to such as were convicted of having plundered the provinces and oppressed the people committed to their care. These he never spared , though his friends , favourites , and kinsmen ; but sentenced them to death , and caused them to be executed , notwithstanding their quality, or former services , like common malefactors. He banished one of his secretaries for giving his council in writing a false account of an affair ; and caused the sinews of his fingers to be cut , that he might never write after. One of his servants , convicted of receiving a bribe , he caused to be crucified on the road which led from the city to the villa where he frequently resided , that , by the sight of the body , which was left on the cross, others might be deterred from the like practices. Eucolpius , the historian , as quoted by Lampridius, informs us , that he could not even bear the sight of such public robbers: insomuch that one Septimius Aribinus , who had been tried for that crime , but acquitted by favour of Heliogabalus , coming one day with other senators to wait upon the emperor , Alexander , on seeing him , cried out with the utmost disdain, « O ye immortal gods ! is Aribinus still alive, and a senator ! does he even presume to appear in my presence ! surely he takes me to be as wicked as himself! » After this he caused it to be proclaimed by the public crier ; that if any one guilty of the same crime ever presumed to appear in his presence, he should immediately receive his deserved punishment, notwithstanding the pardon granted to him by his predecessor. He was sparing of the public money, though liberal of his own. He retrenched all the pensions which Heliogabalus, his predecessor, had settled on buffoons, stage-players, charioteers, gladiators, etc. saying, that the emperor was but the steward of the people, and therefore could not, without the utmost injustice, thus wantonly squander away their revenues upon persons no ways useful to them.

ALEX. VIT. 119.

Tarquinius Superbus ascended the throne of Rome without the observance of any of the laws which till then had been practised ; nor was the royalty conferred on him either by people or senate. His whole reign was almost one continued act of pride,

Q 3

cruelty, and oppression. Such a conduct rendered the people very unhappy, and made them wish for an opportunity of throwing off the yoke. The rape committed on Lucretia, by Tarquin's eldest son, and the sight of her body exposed all over bloody in the forum of Collatia, breeds an universal sorrow, and inspires a lively desire of revenge. Brutus, the father of Lucretia, Collatinus, her husband, and Valerius Publicola, bind themselves by a mutual and most solemn oath, « That with fire and sword they will pursue Tarquin, his wife, and all his guilty race. » The youth first take arms, and being joined by some of the most considerable and most esteemed citizens, the insurrection became general. Brutus, as captain of the guards, (præfectus celerum) ordered a herald instantly to call an assembly, to whom he expatiated on the loss of their liberty, and the cruelties they suffered by the usurpation and oppressive government of Tarquin. He likewise laid before them the reasons of his present conduct, and the designs he had in view for restoring their liberty. The whole assembly applauded the speech, and immediately decreed Tarquin, his wife, and family, to perpetual banishment. A new form of government was now proposed , and after some difficulties , it was unanimously agreed to create , in the room of kings , two consuls, whose authority should be annual. The right of election was left to the people , but they were to be chosen out of the patricians. Brutus and Collatinus were accordingly chosen consuls , who swore for themselves , their children , and posterity, never to recall either Tarquin , or his sons , or any of his family : that the Roman people should never more be governed by kings , nor ever suffer any measures to be taken for their restauration ; and that those who should attempt to restore monarchy should be devoted to the infernal gods , and immediately put to death. But before the end of the year a conspiracy was formed, in which many of the young nobility were concerned ; among the rest were the two sons of Brutus the consul.

The head of the conspiracy appointed a meeting at one of their houses. After supper, and when the servants were dismissed , they openly talked of their project, thinking themselves without witnesses. They were so infatuated by a supernatural blindness , says Dionysius, as to write under their own hands letters to the tyrant , informing him of the number of the conspirators, and the time appointed for dispatching the consuls. A slave, called Vindicius, who suspected something, stood without the apartment, where he heard their discourse, and through a crevice of the door, saw the letters which they were writing. He instantly ran and told the consuls what he had seen and heard. The consuls immediately going with a strong guard, but without noise, apprehend the conspirators and seize the letters.

As soon as it was day, Brutus ascended his tribunal. The prisoners were brought before him and tried in form. Vindicius's evidence was heard, and the letters to Tarquin were read; after which the conspirators were allowed to speak, if they had any thing to urge in their defence. Sighs, groans, and tears were their only answer. The whole assembly stood with down-cast looks, and no man ventured to open his mouth. This mournful silence was at last broke with a low murmur, *Banishment; Banishment.* But unmoved by any motive but the public good, he pronounced upon them the sentence of death.

Never was an event more capable of creating at the same time both grief and horror.

Brutus, father and judge of two of the offenders, was obliged by his office to see his own sons executed. A great number of the most noble youth suffered death at the same time, but the rest were as little regarded as if they had been persons unknown. The consul's sons alone attracted all eyes; and whilst the criminals were executing, the whole assembly fixed their attention on the father, examining his motion, behaviour, and looks, that in spite of his sad firmness, discovered the sentiments of nature, which he sacrificed to the necessity of his office, but could not entirely stifle.

LIV. l. ii. c. 4.

P O L I T E N E S S.

S E N T I M E N T S.

THERE are many accomplishments, which though they are comparatively trivial, and may be acquired by small abilities, are yet of great importance in our common intercourse with men. Of this kind is that general courtesy which is called politeness. I have heard it defined, « an artificial good nature :»

but may we not more truly say , that good-nature is a natural politeness? Art will make but an imperfect work , if the assistance of nature is wanting.

Politeness is that continual attention which humanity inspires in us , both to please others , and to avoid giving them offence. The surly plain-dealer exclaims loudly against this virtue , and prefers his own shocking bluntness and Gothic freedom. The courtier and fawning flatterer, on the contrary , substitute in its place insipid compliments , cringings, and a jargon of unmeaning sentences. The one blames politeness , because he takes it for a vice ; and the other is the occasion of this , because that which he practises is really so.

E X A M P L E S.

Honorius is a person equally distinguished by his birth and fortune. He has , naturally , good sense, and that too hath been improved by a regular education. His wit is lively , and his morals without a stain.

Is not this an amiable character ? Yet Honorius is not beloved. He has , some way or other , contracted a notion , that it is be-

neath a man of honour to fall below the very
height of truth in any degree , or on any occasion whatsoever. From this principle he
speaks bluntly what he thinks , without re-
garding the company who are by : and he
justifies this.

« You may think as you please , says he ,
of my address : my countenance , my attitude , and all those artificial rules of behaviour , which are called civility , I am in no
pain about : I leave these important trifles
to our young senators , or effeminate courtiers. I would have people judge of me by
actions , and not by my gait , for I do not
visit my friends to do honour to my dancing-
master. As to my manner of living with
mankind , I reduce it to this , to speak the
truth , to be serviceable to my fellow–creatures, and never to injure them. These being
my principles , I know how to constrain and
deny myself , if necessary , to do any useful
services. I give my advice when it is asked
in affairs that come within my knowledge :
I freely employ my credit and influence, and
sometimes my purse to assist my friends , or
whoever has need of them ; but I think myself justly dispensed from a frivolous com-
plaisance , which can afford no solid advan-

tage to those who demand it. I seldom praise others, and would never have them praise me, because praise is a kind of poison. I contradict the man who asserts a false fact, or advances a false principle; because he must be a liar, or a deceiver, who will not confute a lie or an error; and this I do with a vehemence that adds a weight to my reputation. The rank of the person I attack encourages instead of intimidating me; because the more considerable the adversary is, the more important it is to humble him. Damon is vain, I mortify his pride: Laura is a coquette, I reproach her with her intrigues; Leander is a hypocrite, I pull off his mask; Bertholda is silly and affected, I rally and mimick her; Cydalisa delights in scandal, I lay open and expose her other faults, in order to cure her of this; Lysimon affects to be thought learned, I examine and disconcert him. »

Honorius, in this portrait, has not belied the frankness of his character; but is not this frankness, for which he professes such a value, carried too far? It is not surely impossible to contradict with respect, and to please without adulation. But what is the consequence of a continued course of this sort of behaviour?

behaviour ? Why he has rendered himself dreaded as a monitor, instead of being esteemed as a friend.

Garcia, on the contrary, came into the world under the greatest disadvantages. His birth was mean, and his fortune not to be mentioned :. yet, though he is hardly forty, he has acquired a handsome estate in the country, and lives on it with more reputation than most of his neighbours. While a servitor at the university, he, by his assiduities, recommended himself to a noble lord, and thereby procured a place of fifty pounds a year in public office. His behaviour there made him as many friends as there were persons belonging to that board : his readiness in doing favours gained him the heart of his inferiors : his respect to those in the highest characters in the office procured him their good will; and the complacency he expressed towards his equals, and those immediately above him, made them espouse his interest with almost as much warmth as they did their own. By this management, in ten years time he rose to the possession of an office which brought him in a thousand pounds a year salary, and near double as much in perquisites. Affluence hath made

R

no alteration in his manners. The same easiness of disposition attends him in that fortune to which *it* has raised him ; and he is at this day the delight of all who know him , from an art he has of persuading them , that their pleasures and their interests are equally dear to him with his own. Who, if it were in his power , would refuse what Honorius possesses ? or who would not wish that possession accompanied with Garcia's dispositions ?

POLITE PHILOSOPHER.

Petrarch relates that his admirable friend and contemporary , Dante Alighieri one of the most exalted and original geniuses that ever appeared , being banished his country , and having retired to the court of a prince which was then the sanctuary of the unfortunate , was held in great esteem ; but became daily less acceptable to his patron , by the severity of his manners and the freedom of his speech. There were at the same court many players and buffoons , gamesters and debauchees ; one of whom , distinguished for his impudence , ribaldry , and obscenity , was greatly caressed by the rest , which the prince suspecting Dante not to be pleased with, ordered the man to be brought before him, and having highly extolled him, turned to Dante and said, « I wonder that this person, who is by some deemed a fool, and by others a madman, should yet be so generally pleasing and so generally beloved; when you, who are celebrated for wisdom, are yet heard without pleasure, and commended without friendship. »

« You would cease to wonder, » replied Dante, « if you considered that conformity of character is the source of friendship. » This sarcasm, which had all the force of truth, and all the keenness of wit, was intolerable; and Dante was immediately disgraced and banished.

But by this answer, though the indignation which produced it was founded in virtue, Dante probably gratified his own vanity, as much as he mortified that of others: it was the petulant reproach of resentment and pride, which is always retorted with rage, and not the still voice of reason, that is heard with complacency and reverence : if Dante intended reformation, his answer was not wise ; if he did not intend reformation, his answer was not good.

ADVENTURER.

R 2

From the foregoing examples we may draw this inference, That he who does not practise good-breeding, will not find himself considered as the object of good-breeding by others: it will therefore be no improper conclusion of this article to give you the character of a complete gentleman, an appellation which ought never to be affixed to any man's circumstances, but to his behaviour in them.

By a fine gentleman, is meant one that is completely qualified for the good and service, as well as the ornament and delight, of society. As to his mind, we must suppose it graced with all the dignity and elevation of spirit, that human nature is capable of; to this we must add a clear understanding, a reason unprejudiced, a steady judgment, and an extensive knowledge. As to his heart, it must be firm, and intrepid, free from all meanness and every inordinate desire, but full of tenderness, compassion, and benevolence; as to his manners, he must be modest, without bashfulness; frank and affable, without impertinence; complaisant and obliging, without servility; cheerful and good-humoured, without noise. In a word, a fine gentleman is properly, a compound of the various good qualities that embellish mankind.   MENTOR.

PRIDE.

SENTIMENTS.

THERE is no affection of the mind so much blended in human nature, and wrought into our very constitution, as pride. It appears under a multitude of disguises, and breaks out in ten thousand different symptoms. Every one feels it in himself, and yet wonders to see it in his neighbour.

The same pride which makes a man haughtily insult over his inferiors, forces him to cringe servilely before his superiors. It is the very nature of this vice, founded on riches, posts, credit, and useless sciences, without personal merit or solid virtue, to render a man as supercilious to those who are below him in fortune, as supple to those in higher circumstances.

Nothing is more manifest than that there is a certain equality to which all men have a natural right, unless it be their meanness to give it up.

Of all human actions pride seldomest ob-

R 3

tains its end; for, aiming at honour and reputation, it reaps contempt and derision.

Titles of honour conferred on such as have no personal merit to deserve them, are at best but the royal stamp set upon base metal.

He that boasteth of his ancestors, confesseth he hath no virtue of his own. No other person hath lived for our honour; nor ought that to be reputed ours which was long before we had a being: for what advantage can it be to a blind man, that his parents had good eyes? does he see one whit the better for it?

It is an insolence natural to the wealthy to affix, as much as in them lies, the character of a man, to his circumstances. Take away, said Lactantius, pride and boasting from rich men, and there will be no difference between a poor and a rich man.

Richness of dress contributes nothing to a man of sense, but rather makes his sense inquired into. The more the body is set off, the mind appears the less.

Pride and ill-nature will be hated in spite of all the wealth and greatness in the world, but civility is always safe.

E X A M P L E S.

While Alexander the Great was at Memphis, he formed a design of visiting the temple of Jupiter-Ammon. This temple was situated in the midst of the sandy desarts of Lybia, twelve days journey from Memphis. The motive of this journey, which was equally rash and dangerous, was owing to a ridiculous vanity. Alexander having read in Homer, and other fabulous authors of antiquity, that most of their heroes were represented as sons of some deity; and, as he himself was desirous of passing for an hero, he was determined to have some god for his father. Accordingly he fixed upon Jupiter-Ammon for this purpose and began by bribing the priests, and teaching them the parts they were to act. It would have been to no purpose, had any one endeavoured to divert him from a design which was great in no other circumstance than the pride and extravagance that gave birth to it. Puffed up with his victories he had already began to assume, as Plutarch observes, that character of tenaciousness and inflexibility, which will do nothing but command; which cannot suffer advice and much less bear opposition

The king being come into the temple, the senior priest declared him to be the son of Jupiter, and asserted that the god himself bestowed this name upon him. Alexander accepted it with joy, and acknowledged Jupiter for his father. He afterwards asked the priest, whether his father Jupiter had not allotted him the empire of the whole world? To which the priest, who was as much a flatterer as the king was vain-glorious, answered, That he should be monarch of the universe. At last he enquired whether all his father's murderers had been punished. The priest replied that he *blasphemed*; that his father was *immortal*; but that with regard to the murderers of Philip they had all been extirpated; adding, that he should be *invincible*, and afterwards take his seat among the deities. Having ended his sacrifice, he offered magnificent presents to the god, and did not forget the priests who had been so faithful to his interest. Swelled with the splendid title of the son of Jupiter, and fancying himself raised above the human species, he returned from his journey as from a triumph. From that time, in all his letters, his orders and decrees, he always wrote in the style following : « Alexander, King, son

of Jupiter-Ammon. » In answer to which , Olympias, his mother , one day made a very witty remonstrance in few words , by desiring him not to quarrel any longer with Juno. Whilst Alexander prided himself in these chimæras , and tasted the great pleasures his vanity made him conceive from this pompous title , every one derided him in secret ; and some who had not yet put on the yoke of abject flattery , ventured to reproach him upon that account ; but they paid very dear for that liberty. Not satisfied with endeavouring to pass for the son of a god , and of being persuaded in case this were possible , that he really was such ; he himself would also pass for a god , till at last Providence having acted that part of which it was pleased to make him the instrument , brought him to his end , and thereby levelled him with the rest of mortals.

Varro apud A. Gell. l. xiii. c. 4.

Menecrates , the physician , who was so mad as to fancy himself Jupiter , wrote to Philip, king of Macedon, as follows : — « Menecrates Jupiter , to Philip , greeting. » The king answered ; « Philip to Menecrates , health and reason. » But the king who understood raillery, and was very fond of it when well applied, did not stop here, but hit upon a pleasant remedy for his visionary correspondent. Philip invited him to a grand entertainment. Menecrates had a separate table at it, where nothing was served up to him but incense and perfume, whilst the other guests fed upon the most delicious dainties. The first transport of joy with which he was seized, when he found his divinity acknowledged, made him forget that he was a man; but hunger afterwards forcing him to recollect his being so, he was quite tired with the character of Jupiter, and took leave of the company abruptly.

ÆLIAN, l. 12. c. 51.

P R O D I G A L I T Y.

S E N T I M E N T S.

A Great fortune in the hands of a fool is a great misfortune. The more riches a fool has, the greater fool he is.

There is more money idly spent to be laughed at, than for any thing in the world, though the purchasers do not think so.

We admire no man for enjoying all bodily pleasures to the full; this may create him envy but not esteem. Such pleasures, while they flatter a man, sting him to death.

We may surfeit with too much, as well as starve with too little.

Let pleasures be ever so innocent, the excess is always criminal.

If we consider lavish men carefully, we shall find their prodigality proceed from a certain incapacity of possessing themselves, and finding enjoyments in their own minds: this loose state of the soul hurries the extravagant from one pursuit to another; and the reason that his expences are greater than another's, is, that his want are also more numerous.

The events of this life are fluctuating and precarious; ought not then some provision to be made for unforeseen losses? Ought you not to extend your views farther than the supply of your present wants? ought you not to lay up something for futurity?

To look no farther than the present moment; to live at random, secure and careless of any future exigencies; to concern yourselves about nothing but what is immediately before you; and in the enjoyment of to-day , to take no manner of thought for the morrow , must inevitably be productive of the most fatal consequences , not only to yourselves but perhaps to posterity ; it may entail misery upon children that are yet unborn.

A little is enough for all the necessities , for all the innocent delights of nature , and it may be justly asserted , *that without œcono-my* , how large soever an estate is , there will still be a deficiency.

> Your portion is not large indeed ,
> But then how little do you need ;
>   *For nature's calls are few.*
> In this the art of living lies ,
> To want no more than may suffice ,
>   And make that little do.

EXAMPLES.

The prodigality of the emperor Heliogabalus was as boundless as his lust ; for in the short time of his reign , he is said to have reduced almost to beggary all the subjects of the empire , and to have left at his death the exchequer quite empty. He suffered nothing to appear at his table but what was brought from the most distant countries at an immense expence. His palace , his chamber

chamber, and his beds were all furnished with cloth of gold. When he went abroad, all the way between his chamber and the place where his chariot waited for him was strewed with gold-dust, for he thought it beneath him to tread upon the ground like other men. All his tables, chests, chairs, and such vessels as were destined for the meanest uses were of pure gold. Though his clothes were exceedingly costly, and beset with jewels and precious stones, yet he is said never to have worn one suit twice, nor ever put on again a ring which he had once used. He was constantly served in gold plate; but every night, after supper, presented to his guests and attendants what had been made use of that day. He often distributed among the people and soldiery, not only corn and money, as other emperors had done, but gold and silver plate, jewels, precious stones, and tickets intitling them to immense sums which were immediately paid. He caused his fish-ponds to be filled with water distilled from roses, and the Naumachia, where the sea-fights were exhibited, with wine. His banquets and entertainments were expensive almost beyond belief, his favourite dishes being tongues of

S

peacocks and nightingales , and the brains
of parrots , and pheasants. He fed his dogs
with the livers of geese , his horses with rai-
sins, and his lions and other wild beasts with
partridges and pheasants. In short , the
whole wealth of the Roman empire, says He-
rodian , was scarce sufficient to supply the
extravagance of one man.

HEROD. p. 569. VIT. HELIOG. p. 102.

Cleopatra, queen of Ægypt, to attach Antony the Roman triumvir the more to her
son and interest , made daily entertainments
during his stay at Tarsus , inviting him and
and the chief officers of his army to partake of
them , and spending on those occasions immense sums of money. In one of these banquets Antony expressing great surprise at the
vast number of gold cups enriched with
jewels which were displayed on all sides ,
the queen told him , that since he admired
such trifles , he was very welcome to them ,
and immediately ordered her servants to
carry them all to his house. The next day she
invited him again , and desired him to bring
with him as many of his friends as he pleased.
He accepted the invitation , and came attended with all the chief officers at that time

in Tarsus. When the banquet was over, and the numerous company ready to depart, Cleopatra presented them with all the gold and silver plate, which had been made use of during the entertainment. In one of these feasts the queen had at her ears two of the finest and largest pearls that ever had been seen, each of them being valued at fifty-two thousand pounds sterling; one of these she caused to be dissolved in vinegar, and then swallowed it, for no other end but to shew the little account she made of such toys, and how much she could spend at one draught. She was preparing in like manner to melt the other, when Plaucus, who was present, stopt her, and saved the pearl, which was afterwards carried to Rome by Augustus, and being by his order cut in two, served for pendants to the Venus of the Julian family.

ATHEN. l. vi. p. 147. PLIN. l. xxxiii. c. 3.

REVENGE.

SENTIMENTS.

WHOEVER arrogates to himself the right of vengeance, shews how little he is qualified to decide his own claims, since he certainly demands what he would think unfit to be granted to another.

The man who retires to meditate mischief, and to exasperate his own rage; whose thoughts are employed only on means of distress and contrivances of ruin; whose mind never pauses from the remembrance of his own sufferings, but to indulge some hope of enjoying the calamities of another, may justly be numbered among the most miserable of human beings; among those who are guilty without reward, who have neither the gladness of prosperity, nor the calm of innocence.

A passionate and revengeful temper renders a man unfit for advice, deprives him of his reason, robs him of all that is great or noble in his nature: it makes him unfit for conversation, destroys friendship, changes justice into cruelty, and turns all order into confusion.

E X A M P L E S.

When Alexander the Great came before the city of Gaza, he found it provided with a strong garrison, commanded by Betis one of Darius's eunuchs. This governor, who was a brave man and very faithful to his sovereign, defended it with great vigour against Alexander. As this was the only inlet or pass into Egypt, it was absolutely necessary for him to conquer it, and therefore he was obliged to besiege it. But although every art of war was employed, notwithstanding his soldiers fought with the utmost intrepidity, he was however forced to lie two months before it. Exasperated at its holding out so long, and his receiving two wounds, he was resolved to treat the governor, the inhabitants and soldiers, with a barbarity absolutely inexcusable; for he cut ten thousand men to pieces, and sold all the rest with their wives and children for slaves.

When Betis, who had been taken prisoner in the last assault, was brought before him, Alexander, instead of using him kindly, as

S 3

his valour and fidelity justly merited, this young monarch, who otherwise esteemed bravery even in an enemy, fired on that occasion with an insolent joy, spoke thus to him: « Betis, thou shalt not die the death thou desirest, prepare therefore to suffer all the torments which revenge can invent. » Betis, looking upon the king with not only a firm but a haughty air, did not make the least reply to his menaces; upon which the king, more enraged than before at his disdainful silence; «Observe,» said he, « I beseech you, that dumb arrogance! Has he bended his knee? Has he spoken but so much as one submissive word? But I will conquer this obstinate silence, and will force groans from him, if I can draw nothing else. » At last Alexander's anger rose to fury, his conduct now beginning to change with his fortune : upon which he ordered a hole to be made through his heels, when a rope being put through them, and this being tied to a chariot, he ordered his soldiers to drag Betis round the city till he died. He boasted his having imitated upon this occasion Achilles, from whom he was descended, who, as Homer relates, caused the dead body of Hector to be dragged in the same manner round the walls of Troy;

as if a man ought to pride himself for having imitated so ill an example. Both were very barbarous; but Alexander was much more so, in causing Betis to be dragged alive, and for no other reason than because he had served his sovereign with bravery and fidelity, by defending a city with which he had entrusted him; a fidelity that ought to have been admired, and even rewarded, by an enemy, rather than punished in so cruel a manner.

Q. CURT.

But let us change this horrid scene, and contemplate an example of revenge as illustrious as it is rare.

Aliverdi, generalissimo of the armies of Abbas the Great, king of Persia, and his prime minister, was as good a general and as able a politician, as he was amiable in the capacity of a courtier. From the constant serenity of his countenance, it was judged that nothing could ruffle the calmness of his heart; and virtue displayed itself in him so gracefully and so naturally, that it was supposed to be the effect of his happy temper. An extraordinary incident made the world to do him justice, and place him in the rank he deserved.

One day as he was shut up in his closet, bestowing on affairs of state the hours which other men devote to sleep, a courier quite out of breath came in and told him, that an Armenian, followed by a posse of friends had in the night surprised his palace at Amandabat, destroyed all the most valuable furniture in it, and would have carried off his wife and children, doubtless to make slaves of them, had not the domestics, when the first fright was over, made head against him. The courier added, that a bloody skirmish ensued, in which his servants had the advantage at last; that the Armenian's friends were all killed upon the spot, but that their leader was taken alive. « I thank thee, Offali,»(1) cried Aliverdi, « for affording me the means to revenge so enormous an attempt. What! wilst I make a sacrifice of my days and my repose to the good of Persia; while, through my cares and toils, the meanest Persian subject lives secure from injustice and violence, shall an audacious stranger come to injure me in what is most dear to me! let him be thrown into a dungeon, give him a quantity of wretched food

(1) The prophet most revered by the Persians next to Mahomet.

sufficient to preserve him for the torments to which I destine him. » The courier withdrew, charged with these orders to them who had the Armenian in custody.

But Alverdi, growing cool again, cried out, « What is it, O god, that I have done ! is it thus I maintain the glory of so many years ? Shall one single moment eclipse all my virtue? that stranger has cruelly provoked me; but what impelled him to it ? No man commits evil merely for the pleasure of doing it : there is always a motive, which passion or prejudice presents to us under the mask of equity ; and it must needs be some motive of this kind that blinded the Armenian to the dreadful consequences of his attempt. Doubtless, I must have injured the wretch ! »

He dispatches immediately an express to Amandabat with an order under his own hand, not to make the prisoner feel any other hardship than the privation of liberty. Tranquil, after this act of moderation, he applied himself again to public business, till he should have leisure to sift this particular case to the bottom. From the strict inquiries he ordered to be made, he learned, that one of his inferiors had done very considerable damage to the Armenian, considering the mediocrity of his fortune ; and that he himself had slighted the complaints brought against him. Eased by this discovery, he called for the Armenian, whose countenance expressed more confusion than terror and passed this sentence upon him :

« Vindictive stranger, there were some grounds for thy resentment; thou didst think I had justly incurred thy hatred ; I forgive thee the injury thou hast done to me. But thou hast carried thy vengeance to excess ; thou hast attacked a man whom thou oughtest to respect; nay, thou has attempted to make thy vengeance *fall upon innocent heads* , and therefore I ought to punish thee. Go then and reflect in solitude on the wretchedness of a man that gives full swing to his passions. Thy punishment , which justice requires of me, will be sufficiently tempered by my clemency ; and thy repentance may permit me to shorten the term. »

T R E A C H E R Y.

S E N T I M E N T S.

OF all the vices to which human nature is subject , treachery is the most infamous and detestable , being compounded of fraud , cowardice , and revenge. The greatest wrongs will not justify it , as it destroys those principles of mutual confidence and security by which society can only subsist. The Romans , a brave and generous people , disdained to practise it towards their declared enemies ; Christianity teaches us to forgive injuries ; but to resent them under the disguise of friendship and benevolence argues a degeneracy , which common humanity and justice must blush at.

E X A M P L E S.

Caracalla , the Roman emperor , sent a solemn embassy to Artibanus , king of the Parthians , desiring his daughter in marriage. Artibanus, overjoyed at this proposal, which he thought would be attended with a lasting peace between the two empires, received the ambassadors, with all possible marks of honour, and readily complied with their request. Soon after Caracalla sent a second embassy, to acquaint the king that he was coming to solemnize the nuptials. Whereupon Artibanus went to meet him, attended with the chief of the nobility, and his best troops all unarmed, and in most pompous habits: but this peaceable train no sooner approached the Roman army than the soldiers, on a signal given, falling upon the king's retinue, made a most terrible *slaughter* of the unarmed multitude, Artibanus himself escaping with great difficulty. Caracalla, having gained great booty by this inhuman and barbarous treachery, wrote a long and boasting letter to the senate, assuming the title of Parthicus for this detestable action, as he had before that of Germanicus, for murdering in like manner some of the German nobility.

UNIV. HIST.

Antigonus finding the country in which he lay excessively wasted, and that it would be very difficult for him to subsist, sent deputies

puties to the confederate army to solicit them , especially the governors of provinces and the old Macedonian corps , to desert Eumenes and to join him , which they rejected with the highest indignation. After the deputies were dismissed , Eumenes came into the assembly , and delivered himself in these words : « Once upon a time a lion falling in love with a young damsel, demanded her in marriage of her father. The father made answer , that he looked on such an alliance as a great honour to his family , but stood in fear of his paws and his teeth , lest upon any trifling dispute that might happen between them after they were married, he might exercise them a little too hastily upon his daughter. To remove this objection , the amorous lion caused both his nails and his teeth to be drawn immediately , whereupon the father took a cudgel, and soon got rid of his enemy.» This, continued he , is the very thing aimed at by Antigonus , who makes you large promises till he has made himself master of your forces , and then beware of his teeth and paws.

PLUT. IN VIT. EUMEN. DIOD. SICUL. lib. II.

T

WEALTH (CONTEMPT OF).

SENTIMENTS.

IF we regard poverty and wealth, as they are apt to produce virtues and vices in the mind of man, one may observe that there is a set of each of these growing out of poverty, quite different from those which rise out of wealth : humility and patience, industry and temperance, are very often the good qualities of a poor man. Humanity and good-nature, magnanimity, and a sense of honour, are sometimes the qualifications of the rich ; on the contrary, poverty is apt to betray a man into envy, riches into arrogance ; poverty is sometimes attended with fraud, vicious compliances, repining, murmur, and dis-content : riches expose a man to pride and luxury, a foolish elation of heart, and too great a fondness for the present world. Upon the whole, riches are the instruments of good or evil, according to the disposition of the possessor ; or in the words of Eucrates, a good fortune is an edged tool, which an hundred may get for one who knows how to use it.

A very rich man may eat his dainties, paint his ceilings and alcoves, in summer retire to his seat, and spend the winter at his town-house, may marry his daughter to a duke, and buy a title for his son; all this is right, and within his compass; but to live content, is perhaps the privilege of other men.

Let us not envy some men their accumu-lated riches; their burden would be too heavy for us; we could not sacrifice, as they do, health, quiet, honour, and con-science, to obtain them: it is to pay so dear for them that the bargain is a loss.

Nothing makes us better comprehend what little things God thinks he bestows on man-kind, in riches and dignities, and other advantages, than his distribution of them, and the sort of men who are best provided.

If he be rich who wants nothing, a very wise man is a very rich man.

If he be poor who is full of desires, nothing can equal the poverty of the ambitious and the covetous.

A wise man will desire no more than what he may get justly, use soberly, distri-bute cheerfully, and leave contentedly. He

T 2

that is in such a condition as places him above contempt , and below envy , cannot , by any enlargement of his fortune , be made really more rich , or more happy than he is.

Riches cannot purchase endowments , they make us neither more wise nor more healthy. None but intellectual possessions are what we can properly call our own. How despicable is his condition who *is above necessity* , and yet shall resign his reason , and his integrity , to purchase superfluities.

The greatest pleasure wealth can afford is that of doing good.

EXAMPLES.

Philopœmen having delivered the Lacedemonians from the oppressions they had long groaned under , they ordered the palace and furniture of the usurper Nabis to be sold , and the sum accruing from thence , to the amount of one hundred and twenty talents , to be presented to Philopœmen , as a token of their gratitude. Deputies therefore were to be appointed , who should carry the money, and desire Philopœmen, in the name of the senate , to accept of the present. And on this occasion it was , says Plutarch , that the virtue of the generous Achæan appeared in its greatest lustre ; for so great was the opinion which the Spartans had of his probity and disinterestedness, that no one could be found who would take upon him to offer the present. Struck with veneration , and fear of displeasing him , they all begged to be excused. At last they obliged , by a public degree , one Timolaus , who had formerly been his guest to go to Megalopolis , where Philopœmen lived , and offer him the present. Timolaus , with great reluctance , set out for Megalopolis , where he was kindly received and entertained by Philopœmen. Here he had an opportunity of observing the severity of his whole conduct , the greatness of his mind , the frugality of his life, and the regularity of his manners ; which struck him with such awe , that he did not dare once to mention the present he was come to offer him ; insomuch, that giving some other pretence to his journey , he returned home with the present. The Lacedemonians sent him again , but he could no more prevail on himself now than the first time , to mention the true cause of his journey. At last , going a third time he ventured , with the utmost reluctance , to acquaint Philopœmen with the

T 3

offer he had to make him in the name of the Lacedemonians. Philopœmen heard him with great calmness ; but the instant he had done speaking , he set out with him to Sparta , where , after expressing the greatest obligations to the senate , he advised them to lay out their money in corrupting and purchasing the wicked , and such as divided the citizens, and set them at variance with their seditious discourses , to the end that , being paid for their silence , they might not occasion so many distractions in the government ; for it is much more adviseable , said he , to stop an enemy's mouth than a friend's ; as for me, I shall always be your friend , and you shall reap the benefit of my friendship without expence.

PLUT. IN PHILOP. LIV. l. 35. c. 28.

A treaty being on foot between the Romans and Pyrrhus , king of Macedon , for the exchange of prisoners , the latter after having given a general answer to the ambassadors , took Fabricius aside, and addressed him in the following manner : « As for you , Fabricius , I am sensible of your merit : I am likewise informed that you are an excellent general , and perfectly qualified for the com-

mand of an army ; that justice and temperance are united in your character , and that
you pass for a person of consummate virtue ;
but I am likewise as certain of your poverty ; and must confess , that fortune , in this
particular alone , has treated you with injustice , by misplacing you in the class of indi-
gent senators. In order , therefore , to supply
that sole deficiency , I am ready to give you
as much gold and silver as will raise you
above the richest citizen of Rome ; being
fully persuaded, *That no expence can be
more honourable to a prince than that which
is employed in the relief of great men , who
are compelled by their poverty to lead a life
unworthy of their virtues , and that this is
the noblest purpose to which a king can possibly devote his treasures.* At the same
time , I must desire you to believe , that I
have no intention to exact any unjust or dishonourable service from you ; as a return of
gratitude , I expect nothing from you but
what is perfectly consistent with your honour, and what will add to your authority and
importance in your own country. Let me
therefore conjure you to assist me with your
'credit in the Roman senate , which has hitherto assumed an air of too much inflexibi-

lity , with relation to the treaty I proposed, and has never consulted the rules of moderation in any respect. I want a virtuous man and a faithful friend , and you as much need a prince whose liberality may enable you to be more useful , and do more good to mankind. Let us therefore consent to render mutual assistance to each other in all the future conjunctures of our lives. »

Pyrrhus having expressed himself in this manner , Fabricius , after a few moments silence , replied to him in these terms : It is needless for me to make any mention of the experience I may possibly have in the conduct of public or private affairs since you have been informed of that from others. With respect also to my poverty you seem to be so well acquainted with it , that it would be unnecessary for me to assure you that I have no money to improve , nor any slaves from whom I derive the least revenue ; that my whole fortune consists in a house of no considerable appearance , and in a little spot of ground that furnishes me with my support. But if you believe my poverty renders my condition inferior to that of every other Roman ; and that while I am discharging the duties of an honest man , I am the less considered , because I happen not to be of the number of the rich , permit me to acquaint you, that the idea you conceive of me is not just, and that whoever may have inspired you with that opinion , or you only suppose so yourself , you are deceived to entertain it. Though I do not possess riches , I never did imagine my indigence a prejudice to me , whether I consider myself as a public or private person. Did my necessitous circumstances ever induce my country to exclude me from those glorious employments that are the noblest objects of the emulation of great souls ? I am invested with the highest dignities , and see myself placed at the head of the most illustrious embassies. I assist also at the most august assemblies , and even the most sacred functions of divine worship are confided to my care. Whenever the most important affairs are the subject of deliberation , I hold my rank in council , and offer my opinion with as much freedom as another. I preserve a parity with the richest and most powerful in the republic ; and if any circumstance causes me to complain , it is my receiving too much honour and applause from my fellow citizens. The employments I discharge cost me nothing of mine , no more than any other Roman. Rome never reduces her citizens to a ruinous condition, by raising them to the magistracy. She gives all necessary supplies to those she employs in public stations, and bestows them with liberality and magnificence. Rome in this particular, differs from many other cities, where the public is extremely poor, and private persons immensely rich. We are all in the state of affluence, as long as the republic is so, because we consider her treasures as our own. The rich and the poor are equally admitted to her employments, as she judges them worthy of trust, and she knows no distinctions between her citizens but those of merit and virtue: as to my particular affairs, I am so far from repining at my fortune, that I think I am the happiest of men when I compare myself with the rich, and find a certain satisfaction, and even pride in that fortune. My little field, poor and infertile as it is, supplies me with whatever I want, when I am careful to cultivate it as I ought, and to lay up the fruits it produces. What can I want more? Every kind of food is agreeable to my palate, when seasoned by hunger: I drink with delight when I thirst, and I enjoy all the sweetness of sleep when fatigued with toil. I content myself with an habit that covers me from the rigours of winter ; and of all the various kinds of furniture necessary for the same uses , the meanest is, in my sense , the most commodious. I should be unreasonable , unjust , did I complain of fortune, whilst she supplies me with all that nature requires. As to superfluities , I confess she has not furnished me with any : but then she has formed me without the least desire to enjoy them. Why should I then complain ? It is true , the want of this abundance renders me incapable of relieving the necessitous , which is the only advantage the rich may be envied for enjoying ; but when I impart to the republic , and my friends , some portion of the little I possess, and render my country all the services I am capable of performing , in a word , when I discharge all the duties incumbent upon me, to the best of my ability , wherein can my conscience condemn me ? If riches had ever been the least part of my ambition , I have so long been employed in the administration of the republic , that I have had a thousand opportunities of amassing great sums, and even by irreproachable methods. Could any man desire one more favourable than that which occurred to me a few years ago? The consular dignity was conferred upon me, and I was sent against the Samnites, the Brutii, and the Lucanians, at the head of a numerous army. We ravaged a large tract of land, and defeated the enemy in several battles. We took many flourishing and opulent *cities* by assault; I enriched the whole army with their spoils; I returned every citizen the money he had contributed to the expence of the war; and after I had received the honours of a triumph, I brought four hundred talents into the public treasury. After having neglected so considerable a booty, of which I had full power to appropriate any part to myself, after having despised such immense riches so justly acquired, and sacrificed the spoils of the enemy to the love of glory, in imitation of Valerius Publicola, and many other great men, whose disinterested generosity of soul has raised the glory of Rome to so illustrious a height, would it now become me to accept of the gold and silver you offer me? What idea would the world entertain of me? And what an example should I set Rome's citizens? How could I bear their reproaches? How even their looks at my return? Those

                                          awful

awful magistrates, our censors, who are appointed to inspect our discipline and manners with a vigilant eye, would they not compel me to be accountable, in the view of all the world, for the presents you solicit me to accept ? You shall keep then, if you please, your riches to yourself, and I my poverty and my reputation. »

DION. HALICARN. EXC. LEGAT. p. 744 — 748.

Valerius Publicola, by the consent of all the Roman people, was the greatest man of his age, and the most accomplished in every kind of virtues; I shall mention only one of them here, far superior to all his most noble exploits of war. This Roman, so worthy of praise, who, supported by three other patricians, had delivered Rome from the tyranny and oppression of the Tarquins, and caused their estates to be sold by auction; who had been four times consul; who by two signal victories, the one over the Hetrurians, the other over the Sabines, had twice in his latter years deserved the honour of a triumph; who, with such favourable occasions, might have amassed great riches, even by methods exempt

V.

from injustice and reproach , did not suffer avarice , so capable of dazzling the eyes and corrupting the heart , to ensnare him. Contented with the moderate fortune he had received from his ancestors , he used no endeavours to augment it. He believed that he had enough for bringing up his family nobly, and for giving his children an education worthy of their birth : convinced that true riches do not consist in possessing great treasures , but in knowing how to have few wants : and that the most precious and most noble inheritance that a father can give his children , is glory acquired by great actions , and the examples of virtue which he leaves them. However , at the time of his decease his little stock of wealth was so far expended, as not to be sufficient to defray the expence of his funeral , which was celebrated with magnificence at the charge of the public. « *Moritur* , *gloria ingenti* , *copiis familiaribus adeo exiguis* , *ut funeri sumptus deesset* , *de publico elatus.* »

What praise , what greatness of soul was this ! He dies poor as the poorest in respect of fortune ; more great , more rich, than the richest in virtue and glory. What a misfortune is it for our age , that examples of this kind are so rare, or rather not at all ! the greatest men endeavour to preserve their memories by titles and riches, which they ardently pursue, in order to leave them to heirs who are often little qualified to keep them alive and represent them.

The Roman ladies renewed, in respect for Publicola, what they had done before for Junius Brutus, and went all into mourning, which they wore during a year, as much affected with his death as they would have been with that of their nearest relation.

PLUT. IN PUBLIC. Liv. b. 11 c. 19.

We scarcely find examples of this nature elsewhere. At Rome, before she was corrupted and debauched by ambition, wealth, and luxury, private persons did not divide their interests from those of the public. They considered the losses of the state as their own. They shared in its misfortunes, as if they had been personal and domestic. Such a disposition constituted the force of the state, united all its parts firmly together, and composed a whole not to be shaken, and invincible. These sentiments, perpetuated in every house by living examples, formed the whole city and commonwealth of Rome, in a manner into one and the same family ; of which even the women made a part , though strangers to government every where else. How much ought we to think this contributed to inculcate the same sentiments early into children , and to form them for zealous citizens , from their most tender years! This is what most merits observation in the constitution of the Roman commonwealth , because this is what formed its peculiar and distinguishing characteristic.

F I N I S.

A Paris, de l'Imprimerie de G U E R I N, rue des Boucheries-Honoré , N°. 937.

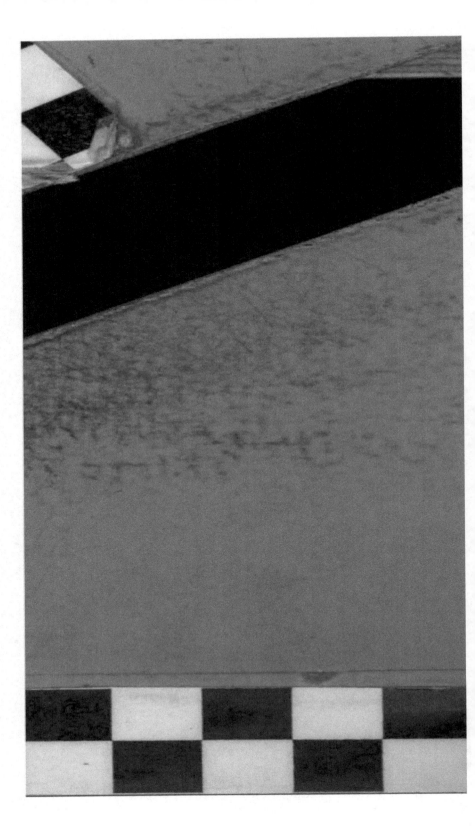

CPSIA information can be obtained
at www.ICGtesting.com
Printed in the USA
BVHW041806220819
556561BV00022B/5290/P